HOW TO SELL BOOKS

BY THE TRUCKLOAD ON AMAZON

BY PENNY C. SANSEVIERI

More books by Penny C. Sansevieri

NON-FICTION

How to Sell Books by the Truckload on Amazon.com
(Amazon Digital 2013)

How to Get a Truckload of Reviews on Amazon.com
(Amazon Digital 2013)

Red Hot Internet Publicity
(Createspace 2013)

Powerful Pinterest
(Amazon Digital 2012)

Get Published Today
(Wheatmark, 2012)

52 Ways to Sell More Books
(Wheatmark, 2012)

Red Hot Internet Publicity
(Cosimo 2010)

Red Hot Internet Publicity
(Morgan James Publishing 2007)

From Book to Bestseller
(Morgan James Publishing, 2007)

Get Published Today
(Morgan James Publishing, 2007)

From Book to Bestseller
(PublishingGold.com, Inc., 2005)

No More Rejections: Get Published Today!
(Infinity Publishing, 2002, 2003)

Get Published! An Author's Guide to the Online
Publishing Revolution (1st Books, 2001)

FICTION

Candlewood Lake (iUniverse, 2005)

The Cliffhanger (iUniverse, 2000)

To subscribe to our free newsletter, send an email to
subscribe@amarketingexpert.com

We'd love your feedback.
Here's how to contact us:

Author Marketing Experts, Inc.
P.O. Box 421156
San Diego, CA 92142
www.amarketingexpert.com

Understanding Amazon

To start off, let's talk about what this book is and what it isn't. Many Amazon gurus out there will tell you that theirs is the quickest, easiest, and most efficient way to make sales on Amazon. And while I don't necessarily doubt their expertise, something I've learned through the hundreds of classes I teach and the research I've done is that if you don't start with a basic understanding of what Amazon is and isn't, your book or product will never gain traction.

Though many experts talk about keywords, categories, and pricing, the one thing that isn't being addressed is the fact that Amazon is less of a store and more of a search engine. And with that model in mind, I need to tell you right up front that there is no instant anything when it comes to ranking on Amazon. Yes, you can tweak your keywords, categories, and themes and see your book sales spike, but the bigger issue is keeping those sales up.

Understanding Amazon and knowing how to use it to your advantage is vital to keeping those sales up. Amazon is *the* place for book marketing today. In an article in June of 2014, SEOMoz, a popular search engine optimization blog, talked about Amazon and their ranking system. They said, "If you're an author you don't care about ranking on Google, you want to rank on Amazon." Everyone in the search engine world knows that several years ago, Amazon ceased being "just a store." Now they are the go-to for anything from books to pet food. And there's another twist: in November 2014, SEOMoz reported on Amazon's new travel service, Amazon Travel. Now, on the surface this seems fairly benign. I mean, so what, right? Amazon sells everything else, why not travel? The problem is that this digs right at the heart of Google's business. Think about it. With Amazon Travel you can get access to the best pricing and possibly the best reviews, which means that sites like Yelp and Google's own review system will start playing second fiddle to Amazon's long-standing and quite extensive review system. And if Amazon Travel is successful, you could go to this one-stop-shop to find everything from a trip to Maui to a contractor for your room addition. Think I'm crazy? Ten years ago no one thought Amazon would sell anything besides books.

What this means, essentially, is that Amazon is gearing up to play a whole different game. That game means more and more people are going to be searching on Amazon. And if it isn't already, Google should be worried.

Thinking in Search-Engine Terms

As you'll see throughout this book, work you do on Amazon is similar to the things I would recommend if you were trying to get traction on Google for your website. This is the mindset you must embrace and something I haven't seen discussed in a lot of the books I've read on this topic. And therein lies yet another problem:

About a year and a half ago there were dozens of these "How to sell on Amazon" books being sold. Now that number has dwindled to just a few. Why? Well, I think a lot of it has to do with the fact that Amazon has changed and continues to change all the time. If you want to stay up on the things Amazon is doing after you've finished reading this book, be sure and subscribe to our blog at www.am-arketingexpert.com/blog, where I regularly post new updates on Amazon algorithm changes and new programs they launch.

The Other Side of Amazon

In addition to the search engine side of Amazon, there is still the store and, as a retailer, Amazon's goal is to sell stuff, and a lot of it. We'll talk more in depth about the retailer part later on in this book, but one thing I've learned is that most authors list their books on Amazon and think they're done. They just assume Amazon will do the selling for them. This couldn't be further from the truth. There are certain strategies you must implement before you can relax a bit.

Aside from being a great place to sell your book, Amazon can be an author's best friend with a little bit of know-how. There is the mysterious search engine component I will unravel for you shortly, but there's also the brick-and-mortar type model Amazon feeds into. Let's say you're a manager at a clothing store, and one day you start to see that cashmere sweaters (last season's style) are selling. Normally you would never put them at the front of your store; you leave that area for the "known hits," meaning the most trending products you know will sell well, right? But when something you hadn't expected to sell at all starts gaining interest, you figure it's a good idea to give it more exposure, so you put it a bit closer to the front. Now the sweaters are selling even faster. So you move them to one of the front tables. Bingo! You sell even more. Then one day when you're redoing your storefront window, you think: *Let's display them here.* Suddenly your stock is sold out. This is, essentially, what happens with Amazon, except replace the sweater with your book. When your book starts selling on Amazon, this superstore takes notice and your book starts popping up in all sorts of places that relate to book recommendations.

If you own a Kindle, you know that when you're looking to buy a book or have just finished reading one, the system shows you "other books" on the same or similar topics. Have you ever wished to see your book there? This is one of the many ways Amazon pushes a book that's selling or showing great promise. How exactly does this happen, and how can you make it work for you?

That's where this algorithm, search engine model and book come into play. What I'll show you relates to algorithm triggers within Amazon's search function. Everything I recommend in this book is free and will cost you only in research and tracking time. Some things I show you may have immediate results, as I mentioned earlier in this chapter; others will take a bit of time. Once you implement these strategies, however, it's a bit of "set it and forget it," meaning that once you've done the footwork, the algorithm kicks in, Amazon does the rest.

Almost 100 percent of the time, when I look at Amazon author profiles, I find that authors aren't doing anything to significantly promote their titles. So many of your book promotion tasks require your own "marketing muscle." Much of that marketing muscle is really marketing know-how—a skill most of us aren't born with. Regardless of the age of your book, if your subject matter is still relevant, you can boost it on Amazon using these techniques. I've seen it happen with books that are five years old. So if you're reading this wondering if you can make this work for your book, I can assure you it can.

What Publishing Looks Like Now

On average, thirty-five hundred books are published *each day* in the United States, and while that number is staggering, it's not even close to being accurate. Why? Because that number only includes ISBNs registered in the system. It doesn't count books uploaded straight to Amazon using their internal ASIN number. The number of books published daily probably looks more like forty-five hundred. Think about that for a minute. What does a staggering amount of books published daily do for your title? Well, for one thing it makes it harder to find. So putting effort into your Amazon page is crucial, but also consider whether or not having only one book out there is enough to draw attention to yourself and your brand.

In addition to talking about Amazon's algorithms, in this chapter we'll look at a few other success strategies you may want to incorporate in your marketing plan.

Short Is the New Long

In most cases, having one book isn't enough to gain traction because often your first book is your loss leader. It's hard to hear, but it's true—at least in most cases. And while your book may be the exception, I've seen that having multiple books out there is a smart idea. If the thought of publishing multiple books is discouraging to you, consider this: the books don't have to be long. I mean, take a look at the two books in this volume. Separately, these titles are between seventy- and eighty-some pages each. Not terribly long, right? Short is the new long. I've spoken to a number of fiction authors who've said their fifty-page novellas are doing better than their longer counterparts. Shorter books are selling. What this means is that you could release one long book a year and then a few novellas or shorter nonfiction how-to guides, manuals, etc. As long as they're relevant, helpful, and/or entertaining, there's no reason they can't be sold, which will help enhance your bookshelf presence on Amazon.

The Age of the Book Bundle

I was at a writers' conference recently and spoke with a guy who told me how his 330-page science-fiction book had been out for a while but hadn't done well. I suggested he split up the book and rerelease it as a series and a bundle. Some folks like shorter books. It's a great way to start owning the virtual shelf. So divide up that longer book, making sure you chop it at natural ending points, and then put these separate segments on Amazon. With a book as long as Sci-fi Guy's, you could create three separate ebooks. Make sure you have a page at the back of each book that leads the reader to the next book in the series. Splitting up your books and bundling them will also revive your publication date and bring it current. It will open up options for promotion and reviews, too.

Combining Forces

We're seeing authors collaborate on a book bundle. In fact, even big-name bestselling authors are doing it. We saw this in 2014 with editor David Baldacci in the book series FaceOff. With the rising popularity of the book bundle, I think we'll see a lot more of this. In fact, I've talked with a few authors who are combining their titles with other authors' titles just to keep putting new titles out on Amazon. With all the new books out there, it's going to be important for authors with a strong following to support each other by combining books and perhaps even combining book tours.

In addition to novellas, book bundles, and different authors combining their efforts, we're seeing more audio books on the market. Offering your books in a variety of formats will be important going forward.

The Surge of Audio and Print

While ebooks will continue to be popular, authors who have gone exclusively to ebooks will find that in order to stay competitive, it's important to make their books available in multiple formats. It's never a bad idea to have a book in print. In fact, if you want to succeed in spite of the deluge of new titles published each year, it's wise to have your book in print *and* in audio format. Audiobook popularity is growing rapidly, with new titles emerging from this channel all the time, including a lot of indie titles previously available in ebook format only. As indie publishing continues to grow, books available in multiple formats will stand out from those in ebook format only.

The Bar is Officially Raised

It's here—that raised bar we all keep talking about. With the hundreds and thousands of books now published, many (more than ever) will go unnoticed. Right now the average sale for a self-published book is one hundred copies. I predict that number will drop to ten or less. Shocking? Not really. A lot of authors aren't prepared for the marketing or the work it takes to get their book out there. Now, more than ever, you'll need not just a good product but an outstanding one. One of the reviewers we work with said the biggest reason she turns down a book is because it lacks good editing. Many indie titles suffer from this, unfortunately. The days of shortcuts, self-editing, and self-designed covers are gone. Bring your A-game or don't play at all.

Street Teams and Super Fans

Now, more than ever, it's important to engage your fans. A few writing events I spoke at talked about "street teams," but "super fans" means the same concept: getting fans to help you sell books. I mention both here so you'll know the terminology when you hear it.

So, how do you make this strategy work for you? First, you need to make your readership feel important. Make them feel as though they matter greatly to the success of the book (because they do!). Offer them exclusive specials and incentives. Remind them often that they are important to you and offer them free "swag" to share with their friends (other readers). One of the authors at Romance Writers talked about how she has a reader who owns a hair salon.

This author sent sample books, bookmarks, and other swag for her friend to put in the shop. This has gone over so well the salon owner keeps asking for more. Be creative with your street teams, and if you need help with something, ask them. You'll be surprised how quickly reader/author bonds are formed and how readers who love you are willing to go the extra mile.

How to Research Keywords

When you built your website, your web designer most likely asked you about keywords. You probably had no idea what keywords were unless you were a keyword expert or had someone helping you, and odds are you gave your designer a blank stare. Maybe you offered them a few keywords you thought were good, but in all likelihood, the words you came up with probably weren't helpful.

When we talk about keywords, think in terms of keyword strings, because that's how people search. Consider the last search you did on Google. Did you hop over to the search engine and pop in one keyword like *mystery* or *romance*? Likely not. You probably plugged in a string of keywords like "most romantic weekend getaways" or "best mystery dinner theatres." Whether you're talking about Google or Amazon searches, they both respond better to keyword strings as opposed to single keywords.

Just about everything we'll talk about in regard to Amazon ties back to your keywords, which is why I want to include a discussion early on with a chapter that unravels this often-mysterious concept. You'll likely refer to this chapter often, as various places in the book will tie back to it.

AMAZON TIP!

Since you're allowed up to seven keyword strings when you upload your book to Amazon's Kindle Direct Publishing (KDP), I suggest you find a minimum of fifteen keyword strings as you're doing research so you can swap them out and/or use them in your book description, etc.

Different Ways to Search

In the next few pages, we'll talk about a few different ways to find keywords. How you search for these will largely depend on your genre, but in any case, you'll want to be sure and play around with your keywords to see what "gels" online. If you've written nonfiction, you'll want to perform general online keyword searches. For fiction, you'll want to stick with searches on Amazon.

Building Ideas

It always helps if you know the keyword your audience will gravitate to. If you don't (and this often happens with nonfiction authors), you'll want to start by digging into search patterns online.

There are a number of keyword search tools (see below), but my favorite is Ubersuggest. Ubersuggest spiders Google daily for search patterns. Take a look at what happens when I plug the term "book marketing" into the Ubersuggest search bar:

book marketing +

- book marketing services
- book marketing plan
- book marketing ideas
  - book marketing ideas
  - free book marketing ideas
  - creative book marketing ideas
  - unique book marketing ideas
  - children's book marketing ideas
  - best book marketing ideas
  - book marketing campaign ideas
  - online book marketing ideas
  - cheap book marketing ideas
  - clever book marketing ideas
- book marketing companies
- book marketing plan template
- book marketing international
- book marketing plus
- book marketing network
- book marketing strategies
- book marketing plan example

book marketing + a

- book marketing agencies
- book marketing and promotion plan
- book marketing and promotion
- book marketing and distribution
- book marketing adelaide
- book marketing australia
- book marketing awards
- book marketing association
- book marketing amazon
- book marketing alliance

book marketing + b

- book marketing buzz blog
- book marketing blog
- book marketing budget
- book marketing best practices
- book marketing buzz
- book marketing books
- book marketing basics
- book marketing business
- marketing book by philip kotler
- marketing book by philip kotler pdf

It delivers an A-to-Z listing of what consumers have searched for in the past twenty-four hours. This is an incredible tool for gauging what folks are searching on and what may be trending in your market. And here's a tip: If you're ever at a loss on what to blog about, do a quick search on Ubersuggest to see where consumer interest is. Often this will give you some great blog-post ideas. Below are the URLs for Ubbersuggest and a few other free keyword search tools:

- Ubersuggest – http://ubersuggest.org/

- Wordtracker – https://freekeywords.wordtracker.com

- SEO Book – http://tools.seobook.com/keyword-tools/seobook/

- WordPot – http://www.wordpot.com

Quick and Easy Keyword Basics

If you're reading through this chapter thinking, "Well, this is fine, but I'm not even sure what my keywords are to begin with," then let's look at some ways to help define these for you.

- **Google Analytics:** This great tool helps you find the phrases and topics already driving traffic. Here's how to find your keywords in Google Analytics: Under Standard Reports, click Acquisition, then click Keywords and Organic. This will show you how folks are finding your site.

- **Google Suggest:** Simply begin entering relevant keywords into Google and see what phrases Google suggests. You may also want to use a question opener like "how to" or "what" and add in your topic. The top searches that come up typically have high volume and should give you a good sense of what consumers are looking for.

Amazon's Search Function

Within the Amazon system, there's a search function similar to Google Suggest. But there's a right way and a wrong way to use it.

First off, this suggest feature is good to use whether you have a fiction or nonfiction book, but if you're a fiction author, your most effective way to find search patterns will be on Amazon. Take a look at the screenshot below. I've typed in "selling books," and Amazon's top suggestions for this particular keyword string are:

This is where things start to really heat up because these search suggestions from Amazon will show you the trending interest among their consumers. And if you click on one of the search terms like "selling books on Amazon," it will take you to this page, where you'll see another trick to get more visibility:

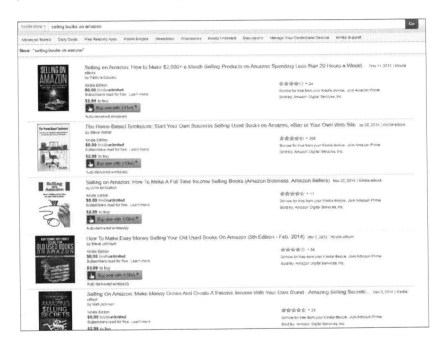

Several of these authors have included the popular search term in their title, which also helps with their ranking. If your book is already finished (and likely most of you reading this are in this boat), then don't worry because there are a lot of other things you can do to help spike your book sales that don't involve changing the title. But if you haven't put a name on your book yet, you may want to think about using this method to find some hot, trending keywords on Amazon!

More Unique Ways to Search

If you've tried to find something on Google, you have, most likely, searched using a search string that involves the word "and"; for example, "mystery and book," or something along those lines. The same type of search string works on Amazon, but there's a bit of a twist to it. Let me show you what I mean.

Let's say you wrote a romance novel and you're trying to find out what folks are searching for. Head on over to Amazon and type in "romance and" and see what pops up:

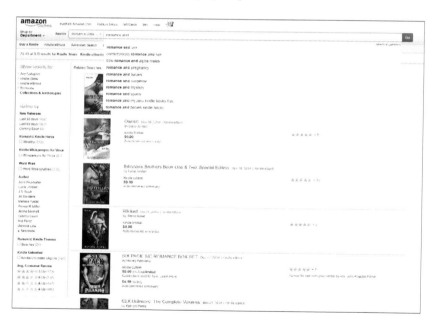

These are autosuggestions based on your keyword plus the word "and." Now let's take this a step further. Let's add the beginnings of another letter to this, creating a search string that looks like this: "romance and c." Take a look at the screenshot below:

You can see that doing this brings up even more search suggestions—see the search string "romance and Christmas"? Fiction authors, particularly romantic fiction authors, take a page from the Hallmark Channel and make sure to incorporate the search term "romance and Christmas" if your book is set around the holidays, because all you have to do is flip through the TV listings to see that, starting at Thanksgiving, Hallmark goes all romance and Christmas all the time. It's big business for them and should be for you too. Though it doesn't typically happen in fiction, it's a good idea to remember that there are certain keywords that change seasonally. Seasonal tie-ins to your topic should be factored into the keyword string only as long as that string is getting enough searches, which we'll cover next.

Finding Keywords with the Highest Searches

As you start searching for keywords, it's important to know that beyond being a popular search term on Amazon, the ideal keyword string also leads you to books that are making sales. Surprisingly, not all keywords (even those that come up high on Amazon) are terrific funnels. Why? Because though they may be searched on, they may not have the types of books a consumer is looking for. A lot of times this happens when books are populated to a particular category that does not get heavy traffic. The suggestions that pop up on Amazon are suggestions based on frequent searches. This does not necessarily mean they have a high frequency of search or a lot of folks looking at that category, it just means they are being searched enough to show up in the algorithm. Let's look at how you can determine if a keyword string is right or wrong for your book.

Let's say you have a military romance book, so you go onto Amazon and type in "romance and military." If you click on the first few titles, you'll see they have a high sales rank:

Sales rank indicates where a book's sales are in relation to other books' sales. A book at number one has sold the most. So a high sales rank isn't good. A book that ranks at 88,453 means that 88,452 books are selling better than that book. A great low sales rank is ten thousand or less, ideally. But this also depends on the genre to some degree. When I've looked at books with the same sales rank, the number of books sold for that particular sales rank varies depending on the genre. For example, a sales rank of thirteen thousand may not seem great, but for some of my own nonfiction stuff, it does pretty well, and in some cases I'm doing $500 plus in book sales at that sales rank per month. However, when I look at that thirteen thousand in fiction, the sales are often lower. So anything you've heard about how sales rank works should be taken with a grain of salt because the numbers vary depending on genre.

That being said, you want to look for keywords that support two things. First, you want to look at whether the search term carries a lot of results. The number of books for each particular search term is located at the top of the page. See the arrow below:

The general rule about the ideal number of books for each particular search term is that you want a low number so you have a better chance of getting to number one. While that's true up to a point, there's something else you should consider. For some categories you may find a small number of books, but the sales rank on the books is pretty high, generally in the one hundred thousands. This means that, yes, there are a small number of books under that search term, but they also aren't selling. The flip side of this is that you may say, "Well, I'll put my book in there and get to the number-one spot with little or no effort." I thought that, too, and shifted a romance book into a narrow keyword string. The book fell like a rock in the rankings, which points us back to the fact that even if Amazon suggests the keyword string, you still need to do your homework and make sure it's the right segment for you.

Quick side note: On our example search of "military and romance," I mentioned that the first few titles weren't great in regard to sales rank. Take a look at the covers. They weren't stellar either. In most cases they could have been better. So why did these titles rank so high if the covers weren't great? I'm betting they tinkered with the keywords in the titles. As you'll see, the book titles and subtitles have a lot of extra words added. Have another look at that screengrab:

But don't discount a good cover. In most cases your cover greatly contributes to whether someone clicks on your book or not. Farther down the list, we see the *SEALs of Winter* superbundle:

And when we click on it, we are taken to this page. Take a look at that sales rank!

Despite the fact that the first few books had sagging sales ranks, the fourth book down on the list was doing really well, as were all the books that followed it.

Now that you know a little about the different ways to search keywords, depending on your genre, you may want to try them all. But remember, if you decide to change up your keywords, be sure to add them to your book description and maybe even incorporate them in your title if your book's not "on the shelves" yet. And make sure someone is actually buying the books you're looking at for keywords. Check the sales rank and make sure it's not too high. With this knowledge of the tools for searching keywords and how to use them, you can implement that knowledge as you get ready to produce a book that will sell.

Creating Bestselling Book Ideas

It's one thing to write a book; it's quite another to write a book that will sell. We all want to follow our passion, write our dream, and dance creatively with our muse, but wouldn't it be fantastic if, amidst all of this creation, we also managed to produce a bestselling book? That is, after all, the dream. This chapter discusses in detail several things you can do to ensure your book targets the largest audience possible.

Finding Bestselling Book Ideas

I know this gal who's keyed in to a bunch of SEO people. For those of you not familiar with the term, SEO stands for "search engine optimization." These are the folks who spend their life trying to get on the first page of Google. Several years back, she and I were talking about how to create ideas that sell. She told me that many of her SEO buddies write books literally just based on keywords. It has nothing to do with their passion or what they really even want to write about. They focus on saleable terms, meaning phrases getting a huge bounce in Google. This may not be how you'd normally consider writing a book, but there are merits to this methodology. Here are a few things to consider as you contemplate what to write about:

- **Book focus:** Where will you focus your book? Don't get too caught up in a set plan. Leave some room for flexibility and consider what's "hot" right now. What is an immediate need? You may still stick with your original plan but slant it a bit toward what's hot in search.

- **Book title:** As mentioned previously, this is a great place to use keywords.

- **Book subtitle:** If you already have your title, consider using keywords in your subtitle to help boost your exposure in search.

- **Book topic:** Let's say you're an expert in your field but aren't sure what to write about. Let's say you're a consumer finance guru and want to write a book on this topic. Knowing what consumers are searching on as it relates to finance is a great way to key in on the immediate needs of your readers. Create a topic that's narrower. Instead of addressing a broad area, focus in more granularly. This will net you better sales. Consumers like specialized topics that help solve specific problems. And the books don't have to be long. Once you find this market or niche, you'll want to publish regularly to it.

Now, let's assume you've done the keyword research suggested in this book. Let's see how these searches relate to popular topics on Amazon.

Give this a try:

1. On the Amazon page, search the Kindle store tab. Isolate your searches there for now.

2. Plug in your search term and see what comes up. You'll generally get five to ten suggestions. Click on one of them.

3. Look at the books that come up in the search and click on the "customers also bought" section.

4. Focus on books with a low sales rank. Depending on the category, it could be as low as 20,000 or as high as 50,000.

5. Make sure there's a variety of books in the "also bought" section, preferably more than five (around the same topic), and that they all have this range of sales volume. If it's lower than 20,000, that's great, but neither the super-saturated or unpopular categories will help you.

Some Amazon experts say a 20,000 rank indicates the book is selling five copies a day, but I find this hard to prove either way. Just know that given Amazon's volume, it's definitely not languishing at that rank.

In addition to topic research, when you're developing your book idea and trying to decide what to include and exclude, consider spending a bit of time comparing the content of other, similar books in your market. Take advantage of Amazon's "look inside the book feature" and read several pages as well as the reviews. Readers will tell you what they want, and they'll often do it in a review. The negative reviews with constructive feedback—those with what readers thought was missing or things they wished had been expanded upon—will be particularly helpful.

Staying on the Short and Narrow

While full-length books will never go away, there's a trend toward shorter, niche books—books that "own" a narrow market segment. When I first published *How to Sell Books by the Truckload on Amazon*, I was surprised at how its sales outpaced my other books. While I know the title had a lot to do with this, the book was shorter and focused on one particular area. Keep in mind that if you do short, you don't have room for fluff. You'll want to be crystal clear on specific instructions, maybe even including step-by-step instructions or checklists, which readers love.

So, how short can short be? Ten thousand to seventeen thousand words is generally acceptable. Anything under fifty pages is too short; sixty-five pages is a safe bet, but be cautious in preparing your final content. If your book is too short, Amazon's "look inside the book" feature will reveal most of the book, or enough that readers may glean what they want and not buy it. If you've finished the book and it seems a bit too short, consider adding things like checklists, free resources, or bonus chapters from other books you've written that relate to the topic. Of course, don't plump up your page count just to plump it up. Make sure that if you need to add pages, you are adding helpful, useful information. If the book is too much like a white paper instead of a book, you may end up with a lot of window-shoppers who don't end up buying. And while short is the new long, if you do decide to write shorter books, don't be exclusive about it. Mixing it up is the best track for success.

Keyword Strategies for Greater Visibility

I mentioned earlier how Amazon's algorithm is somewhat similar to Google's. When you want a website to rank on Google, you need a good set of keywords on the homepage, ideally in the copy. It's also smart to have keywords in your website address to boost your visibility in search. Though Amazon responds differently, the idea is still the same.

First, let's take a look at the three keys of Amazon ranking:

- Popularity of your title

- Matching search term

- Social proof/reviews

I'll show you how to hit each of these algorithm triggers shortly.

There are approximately one billion ebook titles and three million print books on Amazon, and yes, you can still be on page one or claim the number-one title. Why? Because most people aren't aware that Amazon is its own search engine. But now that you are, you can use that information to your advantage. Keep in mind that the tools shared in this book won't guarantee your book the number-one spot on Amazon, but it will get it a significant amount of attention. And in the end, isn't that what we want?

Understanding Metadata

At one time, no one talked about metadata. Now it's the hot, new buzzword. Essentially, metadata refers to the keywords, categories, and (in some cases) tags, but Amazon got rid of book tagging awhile ago. Zeroing in on Amazon's metadata is a fantastic way to gain more attention for your book, and the great thing is that everything counts. Your book title, subtitle, keywords—all of it matters. Let's take a closer look at metadata so you can see what I mean.

Making Your Book More Searchable

The more searchable your book is, the more often it's going to come up in searches, and consequently, your sales will increase. Part of this is Amazon's metadata, which is accessible to any author who has their book on Amazon, but most authors and publishers don't use it or understand it.

KDP, Amazon's Kindle Direct Publishing program (and their ebook partner), is a popular way to get your book onto the Amazon platform. If you publish on Amazon or on KDP, there's a place to type in keywords. Take a look at this screenshot of the dashboard for the KDP site, where you access each of your book's features.

You can see that you're allowed up to seven search keywords, and though Amazon says it's optional, it really shouldn't be. As I was doing research for this book, I asked ten authors to let me take a look at the back end (behind-the-scenes) details of their book with the caveat that I wouldn't add terms they didn't need. *None* of them had search words listed. Categories are always a given—all my authors had chosen their categories—but search keywords are often ignored. Start thinking about your keywords, because they matter—more than you know. Remember not to get stuck on single words. You can have entire keyword strings, as you see in the screenshot above, and yes, you should use all seven strings.

Monitoring Keywords

Once you've selected your keyword strings, it's important to continually monitor them. You may not want to stick with the same keywords for the duration of your book's life on Amazon. Why? Because search habits change, some searches are more popular than others, and you won't know which will get you the most bounce until you start playing with keyword terms. I recommend you start a spreadsheet with the various keywords you've selected for your book and keep track of where your book is ranking whenever you search these terms.

Do not, under any circumstances, use anything other than standard words and phrases for your keywords. You can use keywords like "romance," "contemporary romance," and even things like "kindle deals under $3.99" (as long as your book fits that pricing), but you can no longer use author names and/or book titles. This is significant because it's been a popular marketing strategy for ages among authors and publishers. It's the old "If you liked that, you'll love this!" model. Aligning your book to a reader's tastes is what you want to do, but Amazon now prevents it. One book actually was pulled of the "shelf" by Amazon for using the wrong keywords, so beware.

Read more about it here: http://www.amarketingexpert.com/author-alert-resolving-amazon-keyword-issue/

Simple Keyword Success Strategies to Rock Your Book

Now that you understand where your keywords come into play in regard to your Amazon back end, let's take a look at the other ways you can use them.

Titles and Subtitles

The title of your book can often make or break its success, but most authors have not considered adding keywords to their title and/or subtitle. Many times, particularly in nonfiction, I see authors give their books nebulous titles. This is a mistake, especially with all the titles on Amazon and all the books your reader has to choose from. For those of you who haven't titled your book or are coming out with a second or third, think about using keywords for your title. If your keywords aren't going to work with your title, will they work for your subtitle? They will. Subtitle keywords matter, and here's the thing: the subtitle doesn't have to appear on your book; it can simply be part of the Amazon page.

Book Description

The book description, often overlooked as a means to drive traffic to your page, is also a great place to use keywords. A book description should draw the reader in, but authors tend to get too flowery with these. Flowery is fine if you're selling fiction, but even then you can still use keywords in effective ways. Here's a screenshot of this book, *How to Sell a Truckload of Books on Amazon*. You'll see I use keywords throughout the page—in the header, in the description, and in the bullets:

When it comes to fiction, the rules still apply, but you may have to be creative in using your keywords. Let's say you find a series of keywords like this:

- new romance ebooks

- romance and sex

- romance ebooks

- romance and mystery

It's pretty tough to fit these into a general description if you're sharing character details, etc., but you could consider using them as descriptors for your reviews. If your book description is long enough, you could definitely include some of these, but using the entire term "best new romance ebooks" will look awkward. Instead, consider adding it as an additional descriptor to review blurbs. For example,

"Loved this book packed with **romance and sex!**"

"Fantastic buy and among one of the best **new romance ebooks!**"

Be sure to check with your endorser and ask if it's ok that the review is reworded slightly. Don't redo the entire review; ideally, you should only have to add a word or two to weave the keywords in. Something I've done is add them after the review. If someone writes: "This is a thrill-a-minute ride. I couldn't put it down!" I add, "Sally Reviewer commenting on this **romance and mystery** book." It can look slightly awkward, so you'll want to play around with it till it feels and reads right, but the point is that weaving in as many keywords as possible can substantially help your search rank.

Some SEO people will tell you to use just one string while others say you should cram all of them into your description. As mentioned, for nonfiction this is pretty simple. Fiction is trickier. Use what feels and reads right; don't overstuff your description just for the sake of inserting keywords.

I read one book about Amazon promotion that said you should use the keywords you find seven times. Frankly, I don't think the number of times matters. The nature of the keywords will, so spend your time creating a description that utilizes these terms and presents your book in the best possible light. My sense is that, much like the use of author names in keywords, Amazon will start cracking down on keyword stuffing in the book description too, so be careful!

The Importance of Amazon Categories

The category your book's in is extremely important to the sale of the book. It's more than just where your audience will find the book. The more niched you can get, the better. Some authors look at bigger categories, like business or social media, and think "I want to dominate that category!" That's a great goal, but it's often not realistic. If you can dominate a smaller niche category, it will trigger the Amazon algorithm as well as their internal promotion system. On Amazon, sales breed sales, so the more sales you get, the more sales Amazon wants you to get. Digging into niche categories can be another way to trigger this system.

There's a catch, however. Back in May of 2014, categories started changing, mostly in regard to fiction. Previously you could find a super narrow category like "dramas" under contemporary romance and get your book placed there. All of that has changed. While fiction still has categories, they are more general in nature, and the narrow searches we talked about in the "Keyword Strategies for Greater Visibility " chapter are accessed with the right keywords but also with something called "themes," which we'll discuss later. If you have a fiction book on Amazon and haven't done a lot with it recently, you may want to check which category the book is in. If you've had it in a narrow category, you can bet Amazon moved it.

And here's another twist to the story: Amazon is divided into two websites, and if you're only doing category research on one side, you may be missing out on some great possibilities. Take a look at the first place to find categories.

Here's a full listing of all Amazon categories and their various sub-categories: http://www.amazon.com/-/b/?node=1000

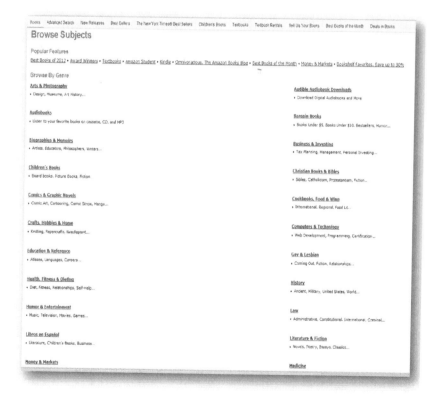

Spend some time researching this list because the more obscure the category, the better. Just make sure it's related to your book; and remember that for fiction you will be using Amazon themes, and not able to go too niche in the category.

Amazon allows you two main categories. Ideally you want to find a narrow niche within these two categories. For example, if you've written a self-help or business book, instead of leaving the book in business or dieting (two super-huge categories on Amazon), you'll want to put it into something slightly more narrow like the subcategory "Women and Business" (which I'll address in a few pages), where it won't get lost in the onslaught of books dominating these markets. You may also want to mix up your markets; consider what other areas your book may do well in. For example, I have a book called *Red Hot Internet Publicity*, which I put in both the business and Internet marketing sections. Readers may search both areas, so I'm covered.

Be aware that categories can change and often do, without notice. Sometimes Amazon even deletes categories. It won't delete your book from the system, but it will delete it from that category and put it somewhere else.

Additional Ways to Find Categories on Amazon

The second side of Amazon has some great additional categories for your book. Here's how to access it:

1. Go to Amazon.com and in the search bar, highlight Kindle Store, as in the screenshot on the following page:

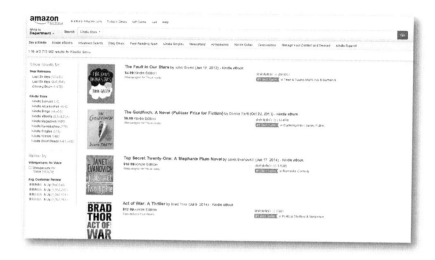

2. Then click Go, but do not put a book title in the search bar. Highlighting Kindle Store and clicking Go will drop you into the Kindle side of Amazon, which has a whole different set of categories.

3. Once you're there, click on Kindle eBooks, and voilà, now you can really start digging around. Don't believe me? Have a look at what I found.

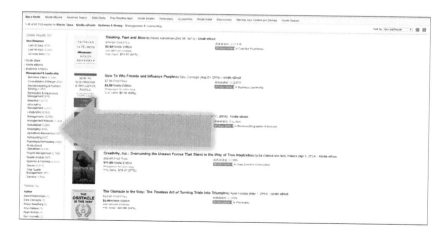

There are a bunch of surprisingly narrow categories like Negotiating, under Business, which has less than eight hundred books in it. Impressed yet? Check this out. Under Business/Business Life, I found the subcategory Work Life Balance, which had only 132 books in it:

Another category was Women & Business, which has a very broad appeal. If you click on this category, you'll see that not all the books are specific to women and business. Though most are written by women, the books' topics range from business success to starting a business.

Changing Your Categories on Amazon

When you first publish on Amazon or add your book to their system, they will ask you for the categories you want your book listed in. Although this is a fairly simple procedure, there's a catch when it comes to categories. Often, authors will add their print book to Amazon (or their publisher will do this for them). Then they'll add the ebook version through KDP. This process is also simple; however, the categories are not the same. In fact, they're very different. In the past, authors assumed their ebook version was automatically listed, but it's not. Thankfully, there's a simple way to change your book category through Amazon Author Central. Let me show you how.

When you've found the right category for your book on KDP, in order to make sure both your print and ebook are in matching categories, you'll need to e-mail the help desk at Author Central. They are super responsive. Here's how to do it:

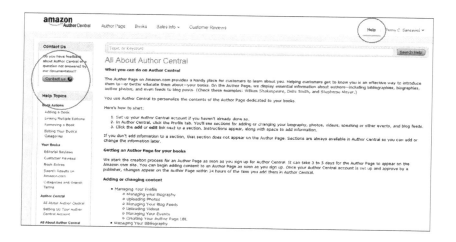

After you click on Help, select Contact Us (both circled in red). Once you get there, you'll click the following in this order:

- My Books

- Update information about a book

- Browse categories

- I want to update my book's browse categories

The page will look like this. Be sure to note that you want e-mail contact.

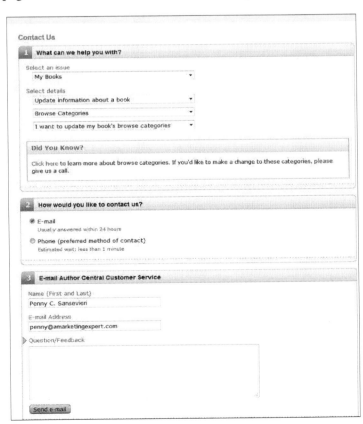

The folks who monitor the Amazon Author Central pages are helpful and efficient. Even if you get the topics you want to contact them about wrong, your e-mail usually ends up in the right place. Once you're on this screen, you'll want to ask them to move your ebook to the category you specify. Sometimes your publisher will do this for you, but if not, it's pretty straightforward.

Amazon Themes

According to Amazon, "themes" were implemented for fiction books because consumers were searching for things like the type of protagonist or where the book was set (beach, city, etc.). It's rumored that Amazon plans to use themes for nonfiction, but as of this writing I have not seen this change implemented. So what are themes? They are the various aspects of your book's content. For example, if you have a wealthy protagonist, one of your themes would be "wealthy." If you have a murder-mystery with a serial killer, your theme might be "serial killer." Here's what themes look like on the Amazon page:

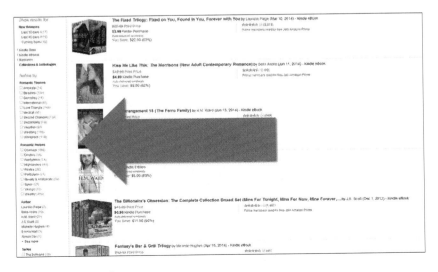

You can see a list of "Romantic Themes" and "Romantic Heroes" on the left-hand side of the screen. If you've written a thriller or mystery, you'll have three choices: Moods & Themes, Characters, and Setting.

Here's where your seven keywords come into play. If your book is fiction, your keywords will also be your themes. For instance, if you have a romance novel, you'll replace two of your keyword strings with your theme. If you've written a mystery, you'll replace three of them. Utilizing themes is, of course, optional, but you can bet that if Amazon is rolling this out, it's probably based on hard data.

I highly recommend using theme words in your book description. If you want to swap out keywords with theme words, you can do this through your Amazon dashboard or ask your publisher to change them if you don't have access to it.

Finally, if you have a KDP account, you can access the keywords Amazon encourages you to add to your book metadata in order to gain visibility for that particular search. I would, however, test these just as you would test other keywords because when I've used them, some work brilliantly while others do not. (Note: this URL only works if you have a KDP account and are logged in): https://kdp.amazon.com/help?topicId=A200PDGPEIQX41

Amazon Book Pricing

Don't forget that when you're promoting your ebook, it's always good to remind people they don't need a Kindle or ebook reader to access it. There are apps for just about anything. Here's a list you can share with your audience: http://www.amazon.com/gp/feature.html?docId=1000493771

Book pricing is another way you can trigger the Amazon system to boost your ranking. First, however, it's important to understand the Amazon royalty system. When you publish through KDP, you can chose either a 35 or 70 percent royalty. Initially you might say 70 percent is a no-brainer. But there's more to it than that. Amazon has a "sweet spot" when it comes to pricing. The highest-rated ebooks are generally priced between $.99 and $2.99. This doesn't mean you won't see higher-priced books in top categories, but they typically will bounce there for a short period of time and then vanish. Consistent sales require better, smarter pricing, especially for first-time authors.

A lot of folks will price books based on word count, and while there's some merit to that, keep in mind that if you price your book over five dollars, you could be pricing yourself out of the market.

How to Boost Your Book with Amazon's Pre-Order

I was excited to see that Amazon now allows pre-orders for KDP authors, which essentially levels the playing field between traditionally published authors and those who self-publish through KDP. I'll take you through the steps to get your book into pre-order, but first let's look at when and how this may benefit you.

On Amazon's Kindle Pre-Order information page, they say that pre-order is great for building buzz. True. But there is a caveat. Over the years I've found that pre-orders aren't as effective when you have no fan base, and even then they're iffy. So what's the real benefit to pre-order? Here's the breakdown:

Newly published: If you're a newly published author, the idea of a pre-order seems super enticing, right? Your book is up on the Amazon site as time ticks toward its release. It's pretty exciting, but don't spend a ton of time marketing to a pre-order page at this point. No one knows you (yet), so any marketing efforts you make may be a waste of time. You can do a small push to friends and family, and to a mailing list if you have one. At this point it's smart to start playing with categories and keywords to see what spikes the book and what does not, so you'll be ready to go on launch day.

Already published: If you have a book out there (or several), and you've built a mailing list of fans, then pre-order can build excitement for your upcoming book. But most, if not all, of your marketing should be reserved for when the book is available on Amazon because that will benefit you so much more. Unless you are JK Rowling or some megabestseller, it's hard to drive significant numbers to your pre-order page. The other issue you run into is if a reader wants something now, they may not want to wait for your book to be ready and could end up buying something else instead. That said, pre-order can be a lot of fun for fans who have been waiting for your next book.

Long versus short: Regardless of the category you're in, don't stretch the pre-order time to the full ninety days Amazon allows, because if you aren't spending a ton of time promoting the book, you don't want it up too long. I'd recommend a month. Also, be sure to hit the deadline you assign the pre-order because once you select it (as we'll see shortly), you can't go back. So pick a date you know you can hit.

Promotion: To promote a pre-order, buzz it to your followers and your e-mail list. Again, if this is your second, third, or fourth book, interest is going to be stronger than with your first. Still, you can start to drive some interest to the book or at least let your followers know it's coming. You can use images on Facebook posts, Twitter updates, blog posts, etc., but make sure it's all part of the entire conversation, not the only discussion you're having with your followers. Meaning don't just spend your time pushing your book to your followers, because that will get old.

Reviews: Keep in mind that readers can't review a pre-order book, so if you're looking to get some early reviews, consider focusing on Goodreads, where you can push for pre-order reviews.

Pricing your pre-order: As mentioned earlier, there's a sweet spot in pricing. I would keep it low, even if you plan on raising it later. You're competing with millions of titles on Amazon and your book isn't even out yet. If you want to entice an impulse buy, keep the pricing low at first; once the book is live you can always raise it.

How to set up your pre-order: First and foremost, you need to be a KDP author. Your ebook should be uploaded into the KDP system via their back-end dashboard. Once you're there, you'll see this:

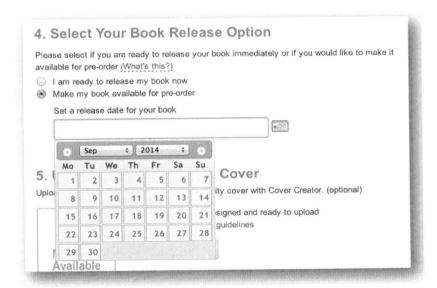

Once you select a date, the system will tell you that you must get the final book to Amazon no later than ten days prior. Additionally, you need to upload a manuscript for them to approve before they'll set up your pre-order. The manuscript doesn't have to be preedited; they just want to see what you plan to publish. You'll need a cover, but it doesn't have to be final, so if you're still a month out with no cover (it happens more often than you think), you can leave it blank or put up a placeholder, then add it later. Here is what the page looks like when it's launched on their site:

According to Amazon, the book can be any length, so if you've written a novella, you can use this, too. Right now there are no limitations other than that you need to be a KDP author and that, clearly, this is for ebooks only.

Pre-order is a fun, cool option for self-published authors, but be mindful of how much of your promotional sweat equity and money you spend. Most readers prefer to buy a book they can get right away.

Five Facts about Kindle Unlimited and How to Make This Program Work for You

Amazon's new subscription service, Kindle Unlimited, is essentially a new way to read a number of books (limited to books enrolled in this program) for one monthly fee. You're limited to ten books at a time. If you want more, you have to return a book or two before the system will let you add more to your library.

Unfortunately, when it comes to nonfiction, Amazon's subscription service is not so great. At least my nonfiction books aren't doing great. It makes sense, though, because Kindle Unlimited speaks much more to the fiction reader, in particular the genre fiction reader, than it does to anyone else. This doesn't mean your book won't do well if you've written nonfiction, but there are some things to consider.

Fact #1: Kindle Unlimited (KU) appeals to the avid reader. This means that if your book is genre fiction, you'll do well here. Hyperfast readers often fall into this category because they can save money with this subscription service. Consequently, some of the highest sales are coming from these readers.

Fact #2: In order to be a part of the KU community, you must have a book enrolled in the KDP Select program. That said, I wouldn't recommend having all of your books in the program at once. In fact, I recommend rotating them in and out of KPD Select. If you have a series, this becomes even more crucial because with KU, if all of your books in that particular series are in the Select program, they will all be relegated to the subscription shelves. Granted, this can work in your favor, but it's smart to keep just the first in the series in KDP Select with a link, letter, or some blurb at the back of the book pointing readers to the next book in the series, and then the next, and so on. Depending on how many books you have in a series, you could conceivably rotate two or three in and out of the program. You'll want to experiment because not all genres (even in fiction) respond the same.

Fact #3: Shorter books rock. I've said before that short is the new long, but that applies even more with your avid reader group. They love the quick read, they read a lot, and shorter books tend to do much better on KU. Also, one of the terms of KU is that you don't get paid until the reader reads 10 percent of your book. For this reason alone it makes a ton of sense to do shorter fiction books. Keep in mind that there are people who try to trick the system by stuffing books with needless content. These kinds of tactics can get your book(s) yanked from the Amazon system. Amazon is onto this and measures actual content. Content triggers in the Amazon system will queue up your file to start the count at chapter one.

Fact #4: When I tested this across a few titles, I found once again that themes matter. Check out this video I made about themes: http://www.amarketingexpert.com/new-keywords-amazon/. Surprisingly, though some are using themes, not everyone is. It may be hard to let go of one or two of the keywords you upload to the Amazon system, but trust me, it will make a difference. In a recent test, I deleted all of the theme keywords taken from the back of a fiction book. The book's sales plummeted, going from eighty-four per week to one. When I reentered the theme words into the keyword area, the book bounced back up again and has returned to almost normal status. It's not yet clear why themes matter as much as they do for KU books, but it's definitely wise to take advantage of them.

Fact #5: Bonus content makes readers happy. An editor will often cut sections from a book. When this happens, authors can create a "director's cut" of the book with the additional pieces either in a separate edition or as separate books on Amazon. Having additional content to drive a reader's interest to your book can be an effective marketing strategy, not just for the KU program, but across the board. If a reader likes your writing, they will likely read everything you've written, and they'll likely tell their friends. Bonus content, director's-cut content—whatever you want to call it—can keep your readers coming back for more as well as pull in new readers.

Fun Amazon Hacks

Amazon Author Central

Every author, regardless of when or what they've published, has an Author Central page. Many authors have not claimed theirs, however. If you're not sure you've claimed yours yet, head on over to https://authorcentral.amazon.com/. You can access it using your Amazon sign-in. Keep in mind that even if you are traditionally published, you still have an Author Central page.

In order to claim the page, you must sign in and add content to the page. First, make sure that all of your books are claimed under your author page. It's easy enough—simply list them in Author Central by inserting their ISBNs and posting them to your page. Amazon will double-check your entries for accuracy, but once they do, you'll find a library of your books on your Author Central page.

In addition to your Amazon US page, you should also check out your Amazon UK page. I don't know why Amazon keeps these separate, but if you grab this page as well, it'll help drive attention from their UK site. You can find it here: https://authorcentral. amazon.co.uk/gp/home. Also watch for Author Central pages for other countries. You'll want to grab those pages as well.

Take a look at this standard Author Central page:

As you can see, this author has added her bio, listed her books, and has book detail pages (which we'll discuss shortly). This works for both print and ebooks—basically any book you have on Amazon can be added to your Author Central page.

Farming Data from Amazon Author Central

One of the bigger benefits of accessing your Author Central page is the data. An author can now get lots of data on their pages, like sales numbers and reviews, plus Amazon keeps adding to this all the time. Let's take look at navigating this page. Below is the top bar you'll see once you log in. From here you can get sales data, rankings for all of your titles, and customer reviews.

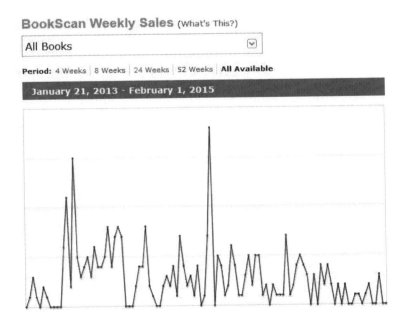

Your sales data is supplied by Bookscan, a reporting agency previously only accessible to publishers or agents. Subscriptions to this service cost a fortune, but Amazon now includes BookScan data in your Author Central page. And even though it's only data for Amazon, it's incredible. You can view sales data for all of your books at once or just one at a time. You can also view this by month and year. You'll want to track this carefully as you do promotions. (The sales data tracked here is for print editions, so if you're published through KDP, you'll have to check your account there to see what your sales are.) Here's a snapshot of what this data looks like at Author Central:

You can also check your author rank, which, unlike BookScan data, encompass both print and ebooks. The rankings can be viewed by month, week, or year. This helps you to see how your rank aligns with copies sold. The mystery remains as to how many copies must be sold to bump up your sales rank, but this information is still helpful.

Adding Reviews to Your Page

Dressing up your Amazon book page is a high priority for authors. Previously, we were at the mercy of whoever reviewed the book on Amazon and whatever details the publisher decided to add. Not anymore. Now you can go in and add your own reviews to help dress up the page. Here's how: Once your books are listed on your page, meaning you've connected them to your account, just click on the book title and it will open to a page that lets you fill in all of the back-end detail. It's that easy. You can do the same with endorsements.

Also, the editing in Amazon is pretty sophisticated, so be sure to bold and underline portions of your reviews (like headlines, names, etc.) whenever possible. It works like Word and makes it easy to draw the eye to a particular sentence or section of the review.

You'll notice that you can also add a book description to this page. I don't know if this is something traditional authors have access to, but I will caution you that this part of Author Central is a bit glitchy. It does not allow you to use more than 480 words or characters. Once you update it on Author Central, unfortunately, you can't go back and change it. Ever. If you want a description longer than 480 characters, you should consider updating your book description else-where. Here's the notice posted in the book description section:

Important: Once you make a change to a section, your publisher will not be able to make any further changes to the same section. Your publisher can still make changes to other sections, but not to that one. If you believe this may cause your publisher concern, please consult them before making changes.

MONITORING REVIEWS ON AMAZON

You can monitor your reviews on Amazon from your Author Central page. A word to the wise: Thank people for their re-views. It's a great way to spread the love and network with read-ers and reviewers. We'll cover more on reviews later in this book.

Favorite Author Feature

Recently, Amazon enhanced the author/reader experience by adding a "Favorite" button to the Author Central page:

Highlight this to your readers and encourage them to make you their favorite. When they do this, they'll automatically be notified whenever you publish a new book.

Enhancing Your Amazon Headline

In addition to farming data, adding reviews and monitoring them, and using the "favorite author" feature, you can add some style enhancers to your headline when you upload your book through the Amazon dashboard. Keep in mind that you can't make these changes through Author Central; it all has to be done from the dashboard. Though this won't affect your algorithm per se, it will help make your book description more visually appealing.

It's the difference between this:

Book Description

Publication Date: **April 3, 2014**

Are you looking for ways to get more honest reviews for your books?

Offering credibility and proof of readership, reviews have the power to boost your book sales. In part two of this book, we share 7 proven ways authors can legitimate strategies we have used successfully to connect with readers and reviewers and now want to share them with you.

7 Proven Ways to Get Reviews

1) Ask Your Sphere of Influence
2) Contact Amazon Reviewers

And this:

Book Description

Publication Date: **February 26, 2014**

If You're Ready to Sell More Books on Amazon, You Must Read This One Now.

Also included, Bonus Book: How to double the amount of reviews you get on Amazon!

Do you know the secrets that can help you sell more books on Amazon?

This easy-to-use guide will walk you through step-by-step what you need to do to kick your book into high gear on Amazon.com

This book is a MUST for any author looking to get more sales and more exposure on Amazon!

⌄ Show more

Here are some of the headline enhancers available:

- Bolding: The text you want bolded

- Italics: <i>The text you want italicized</i>

- Headline: <h1>The text you want for a headline</h1>

- Amazon Orange Headline: <h2>The text you want bolded</h2>

You can add in numbered lists and bullet points, too.

How to Send Even More Traffic to Your Amazon Page!

If you're looking for more great ways to drive traffic to your Amazon page, consider using a URL (web address). You can buy a URL and point it anywhere, so why not to Amazon? Let's say you have a series of mysteries. Your URL might read, "MysteryBooksonAmazon.com." My URL for all of my Amazon books is "SellMoreBooksonAmazon.com." It's been a fun and effective way to drive traffic to my page. I include this URL in all of my books so readers can find other titles if they want to learn more about the ins and outs of Amazon. URL keywords can help bring your books to the forefront.

When you're trying to rank on Google, having the right keywords is paramount. Often we only use these keywords on our webpage, and while this is good, there's another little-known SEO secret you should know about. If you want to rank for keywords, use keywords in your URL. This will help you gain ranking on Google and show up more frequently in searches.

Years ago when I was trying to get more ranking to our main website, AMarketingExpert.com, I bought the URL "BookmarketingAME.com." Since we do book marketing for a living, those are the words we want to rank for. The AME at the end was really more of a place-holder since www.bookmarketing.com was already taken, but the idea here is to find your keywords, ideally two—"mystery books," "romance books," "love and sex,"—and create a URL with them. In almost all cases, the primary keywords for a URL (so, "romance-books.com") will be taken. But you can add to the end of the key-words. For example you could do "RomancebooksAuthor.com" or "RomanceBooksonAmazon.com."

Once you have the URL you want, point your domain service to your book page on Amazon.com. Keep in mind that you can also point it to your Author Central page.

Doing Free eBook Promotions

Promoting your book for free is a great way to boost your exposure on Amazon and help spark the algorithm. Know, however, that not all freebies are equal. By this I mean that it's more important to be strategic than to be fast.

Understanding How Freebies Work

One of the reasons I love KDP Select is that when you do a freebie on Amazon, the system pretty much takes care of it for you. All you have to do is set the dates and hit Schedule. If you're not interested in the Select program within KDP, you can do a freebie outside of Amazon. The Select system within KDP requires you to be on the Amazon site for ninety days, exclusively. Some authors have a problem with that, though I never have. The numbers show that Amazon does the lion's share in book and ebook sales, but if you don't want to be exclusive, then KDP Select may not be for you.

For now, though, let's assume you're in the Select system. During the period your book is free, you'll see the sales rank rise. And even though it's in the free category, it's great because you're gaining traction on Amazon. When your book goes back to paid status, the book will flip to its original category again. It won't keep the sales rank you had when it was free, but it could still be fairly high because most books continue to see a surge when you do a freebie.

Timing Your Freebie

Ideally, you should wait until the book has been up on the site for a while before you offer a freebie. I've found that waiting ninety days is best. You want to give it a chance to grow on its own. As mentioned above, the book will flip from the paid category to the free one and then back to paid once the giveaway is over. Although it ends up back where it started, it will grow because of the residual momentum you'll get from the giveaway. In theory, the longer the book has been on Amazon, the stronger hold it has within the paid category, and the quicker you'll feel the boost as you do this promo.

Pricing and Review Strategies

In addition to timing, pricing and reviewing are two aspects of ebook promotion that can make or break sales.

Generally, I don't recommend starting any type of campaign like this without having at *least* eight to ten reviews on your page. With all the freebie specials being offered nowadays, most consumers won't go for a free book with a naked Amazon page (a page that has no reviews).

Right after the freebie campaign, you'll continue to see a lot of traffic on your page—that residual momentum you've created from the promotion. I've seen it last up to three days. If your book did well during the freebie period, it will help it rise higher in the paid category because it helps trigger the internal Amazon algorithm. The right pricing as it returns to the paid category will help perpetuate this algorithm. If the book did well, it may be tempting to list it at a higher price. However, I recommend you keep your pricing low during the immediate days that your book comes off of free. How low? It depends on how your book is priced in the first place, but generally I suggest you discount it by half for just three days. This may seem counterintuitive; I mean you want sales, right? What better way to sell tons of books at full price by capturing the tsunami of traffic finding its way to your page because of your freebie? You do want to make sales, but don't think short-term. Think long-term. If you can boost your book within a category with the right pricing, it will help to trigger a sales momentum you would never get otherwise, and by keeping your book on your readers' radar screen (by having it show up higher in the category), you'll gain more sales long term.

eBook Promotion

Even if everyone loves free, you can't just put the book up on Amazon, mark it free, and call it a day. You have to promote it.

There are a lot of sites that let you list your book for free (see below), but during your promotion you should be on sites like Twitter, sending messages using hashtags and pinging other accounts. I'm including both the hashtag suggestions as well as some of the Twitter accounts that would love to hear about your freebie.

Make sure you plan your freebie at least two weeks in advance because sometimes listings on sites require that much notice. There are some paid listings too. I've had good success with BookBub.com, Kindle National Daily, and Book Gorilla.

Here's a list of free sites you can list your book on:

- http://katetilton.com/ultimate-list-sites-promote-free-ebook/?utm_content=buffer17435&utm_medium=social&utm_source=twitter.com&utm_campaign=buffer

- www.ereadernewstoday.com

- www.pixelofink.com

- www.peoplereads.com

- www.indiesunlimited.com/freebie-friday

- www.freedigitalreads.com

- www.kindlenationdaily.com

- www.worldliterarycafe.com/content/find-your-books-wings

- www.kindlemojo.com

- www.totallyfreestuff.com

- www.icravefreebies.com/contact

- www.addictedtoebooks.com/submission

- www.kindleboards.com/free-book-promo/

- www.indiebookoftheday.com/authors/free-on-kindle-listing/

- http://www.ebooklister.net/submit.php

- www.kindlebookpromos.luckycinda.com/?page_id=283

- www.thedigitalinkspot.blogspot.com.es/p/contact-us.html

- www.freekindlefiction.blogspot.co.uk/p/tell-us-about-free-books.html

- www.freeebooksdaily.com

- www.freebookshub.com/authors/

- www.frugal-freebies.com

- www.ereaderiq.com/about/

- www.askdavid.com/free-book-promotion

- www.ebookshabit.com/about-us/

- www.ereaderperks.com/about/

- www.snickslist.com/books/place-ad/

- www.awesomegang.com/submit-your-book

- www.goodkindles.net/p/why-should-i-submit-my-book-here.html

- www.blackcaviar-bookclub.com/free-book-promotion.html #.UXFB27XYeOc

- www.kornerkonnection.com/index.html?fb=ebook kornerkafe

- www.dailycheapreads.com

- www.bookgoodies.com/submit-your-free-kindle-days/ highlight-your-free-kindle-days/

- www.indiebookoftheday.com

- www.igniteyourbook.com

Twitter accounts to notify

- @DigitalBkToday

- @kindleebooks

- @Kindlestuff

- @KindlebookKing

- @KindleFreeBook

- @Freebookdude

- @free

- @free_kindle

- @FreeReadFeed

- @4FreeKindleBook

- @FreeKindleStuff

- @KindleUpdates

- @Kindleebooks

- @Kindlestuff

- @Kindlemysbook

- @Kindle_Freebies

- @100freebooks

- @kindletop100

- @kindleowners

- @IndAuthorSucess

- @FreeEbooksDaily

- @AwesometasticBk

- @Bookyrnextread

- @Kindle_promo

- @KindleDaily

- @Bookbub

Hashtags to use

- #free

- #freekindle

- #freebook

- #kindlepromo

- #freeebook

Freebies are a great way to boost your overall exposure on Amazon. They can garner more reviews for the book to help populate the page. I love doing freebies—we've often seen big sales bursts after a campaign has ended.

In addition to offering freebies, you can also promote your book with special pricing. Kindle Countdown Deals offers an opportunity to promote special pricing across a few days. You pick the pricing, and you pick the days. Many of the free sites mentioned above will also let you promote your book if it's ninety-nine cents, which is another great way to get your book out there. Be aware, though, that the idea behind Kindle Countdown is to literally count down via your pricing. If you start the deal at ninety-nine cents, it goes up to $1.99 the next day, and so on until it's back at its regular price. We've found that too many different price points confuse the consumer. Pick one pricing, do the Kindle Countdown, and just let it run for three to five days.

Closing Thoughts

I love discovering new opportunities for promotion on Amazon, and I'm always exploring new ways to get noticed. I hope you've enjoyed part one of this two-book series and that the content benefits you in your Amazon book marketing enterprise. Part two will look exclusively at book reviews and how to get more of them on Amazon—so important to your book. It will help you learn to add more reviews and take your Amazon page to the next level!

Happy selling!

How to Get Reviews by the Truckload on Amazon

Why Are Reviews So Important?

The ebook surge has turned everything on its head. As more and more books hit the market, readers are being deluged with choices, and authors are struggling to get their books noticed. With literally thousands of books published daily, what's an aspiring publisher or author to do? If you want to be head-and-shoulders above the rest, and get your book *discovered*, it's time to get serious about being seen in places your reader will find you. It's time to think about the two things most important to your reader: reviews and engagement.

Why do reviews matter? First, people like what other people like. Second, reader engagement (establishing relationships with your readers through things like reviews, giveaways, blog posts, etc.) drives book exposure and sales. As discussed in the last book, Amazon reviews kick-start your page's algorithm, in turn boosting your book-page visibility.

In this book, we're going to learn how to get more reviews, more readers, and more book sales. It's a lot easier than you think. Marketing people love to complicate the heck out of everything. Well, not all marketing people, but many. And let's face it, there's just a lot of confusing and conflicting information out there.

But let me make you a promise as a person who's been marketing for many, many years. The things you'll learn in this book work. I *guarantee* they do. If the methods in this book don't get you more reviews, more exposure, and more sales, return it to me, personally, for a full refund.

Getting Reviewed

Everywhere you turn, you hear stories about the "shrinking review window." It's tougher than ever to get reviews for your book. And although it's enough to scare off even the bravest of book marketers, it's important enough that my company has become extremely creative—and successful!—in getting reviews.

One of the first things to remember is that it's not so much about who writes the review; it's about who *reads* the review. Too often authors are blinded by names like the *New York Times* and the *Wall Street Journal*, and they overlook publications more suited to their book. Certainly it would be great to get a review in one of the majors, and if your book meets their guidelines, why not? But these national newspapers have thousands of books sent to them each month, and competition is fierce. Search out publications specific to your market and you'll increase the likelihood of getting a review. Don't go after the wrong target. As you're pulling your review list together, dig below the surface. Media is divided into three tiers: national, regional, and trade. Trade media is often the most overlooked segment of a campaign, but there is gold in the trades because the further you go down in the media food chain, the hungrier the media. And that means a greater chance of getting reviewed.

Once you've found an audience to target, take some time to think about your review packet. Are you dressing and stuffing it like a Thanksgiving turkey? Most reviewers don't like fancy folders or a million pieces of paper. And forget food, gifts, and other forms of bribery. They turn a reviewer off. Instead, streamline your review packet. Include a press release, bio, contact info, a fact sheet about the book, a mock review,[1] and a straightforward marketing outline (a single page with bullet points detailing your marketing plans). Including an outline shows the reviewer you're serious about the book's future. If a reviewer gets ten books in a day and can't decide which one to read first, they may pick the one with a marketing plan because the reviewer knows their review (as well as their valuable time) won't be wasted.

Part of the review packet is, of course, your book. Since there's always a chance your book may get separated from your packet, be sure to add your contact information and vitals on the book (pub date, publisher, etc.) to a label, and stick it on the inside cover of your book. That way the reviewer can always return the review to you.

Keep in mind that many reviewers will review only galley proofs, or advanced reading copies, of a book (these are pages printed before the book is bound and published). For print-on-demand authors, you're out of luck unless you get galleys printed several months out. If you're working from a finished book, don't despair! You can still use a finished book for reviews. Just be careful to list the publication

---

1 Written by the author or book-marketing specialist. If a reviewer is pressed for time, they can tweak the mock review and include it in their publication.

date inside the cover jacket (on the label) so that it doesn't obstruct your cover, and include a "galley copy" label on the front cover. These don't have to be special labels; you can print them yourself, but it's pretty industry standard to do this for early reviews. And remember that if you're going after pre- and post-publication date reviewers, you have to honor their timing requirements.

Another way to garner reviews is to search for websites, blogs, or newsletters related to your topic and pitch to them your book for review. The key is to go after a reviewer and target audience with a vested interest in your topic. Pitching to trade media and online media in your specific market will help you increase your chances of being reviewed. It's better to be reviewed in a publication where 100 percent of the readership is your audience than a publication with 1 to 2 percent of your readership.

Though getting reviews is more challenging these days, it's not impossible. With the right target, a streamlined packet, and some online footwork, you can beat the statistics and get your book reviewed. Watch campaign creativity work for you in getting reviews that will help drive interest and sales to your book!

Understanding the Review Process

Over the years, the review process has changed considerably. Years ago when I was first in the industry, there were only two types of reviews: pre- and post-publication date reviews. A publication date for a book was essentially your book's "birthday"—the day it was launched, also called a "street date" or "in-store" date, if you were lucky enough to get into bookstores. Basically, you still have the two types today, but the market has changed, and so *how* you utilize each of them will make all the difference in getting your book noticed.

When a book is published traditionally, the publisher determines the publication date. That date is often a year out because publishers must plan that far in advance. Things just move slowly in the traditional publishing world. If you've self-published, are going to self-publish, or own your own publishing company, you can determine this date, but be sure to leave yourself at least a three- to four-month window for reviews and blurbs and testimonials—prepublication reviews. As you're navigating through various reviewers, you'll see from their submission guidelines how much of a window they want.

Pre-publication versus Post-publication Reviews

Reviews are still divided into these two categories, and though you can do pre-publication reviews, you want to aim for post-publication reviews. These reviews happen anywhere from the day your book is "born" to weeks or months after. Post-publication is where you're golden. While pre-publication reviews are great, major publishers own a lot of this landscape. With all the books big publishers put out there, the field for pre-pub reviews is crowded. Post-pub is a different story. This doesn't mean you shouldn't pursue any pre-pub reviews, just put more effort into what's really going to pay off.

With post-pub reviews, as long as you find reviewers to accept your book, push it as hard as you can for as long as you can. I continue to pitch most of my books months after their publication dates. It's well worth the effort. Remember, it's about discovery. People like what other people like. The more people you get talking about your book, the more people are going to go looking for it.

Advanced Reading Copies or Galleys

In pitching to pre-pub reviewers, you should know some of the ins and outs of the trade. If you're going to push for early reviews, you'll need to get copies of your book printed for mailing. Advanced reading copies of a book are called ARCs or galleys.

ARCs don't have to be perfect. Most advanced book copies include a statement on the cover that says, "Advanced Reading Copy, not for resale," and reviewers know it may still have typos and perhaps not even a final cover. If your book is 80 percent ready, meaning that you're done with the major edits but have one final proofing pass, you can get this draft bound and sent to a reviewer. Your local copy shop can do a tape binding, which is easier to ship than a spiral-bound book. Also, printing off a neatly prepared Word doc is fine; the book doesn't have to be typeset, though I've done it both ways. Ideally, you'll send a final or near-final cover with the book. If you don't have one yet, at the very least send a mock-up.

People often make the process of creating an ARC more complicated than it needs to be. Remember that while presentation is important, it's about the book itself. From a reviewer's perspective, that's how you'll be judged.

If you go with a galley or an ARC, include a sheet similar to the one on the next page. Just insert it at the front of the book. For nonfiction you'll want to provide a brief description of the book and a clear outline of its benefits. For fiction, just the description is fine. Be sure to include any early endorsements you've gotten for the book, too.

Most bloggers post their blog policies and genre preferences—it's important to read their policies in order to understand how long they may need to review your book. If you're working on a tight time frame and they indicate it could take six months to get to your book, you probably won't want to pitch to them. Then again, if your book is in a small niche and this blogger and site seem perfect for you, a longer wait may be worth it.

PENNY C. SANSEVIERI

From Book to Bestseller

An Insider's Guide to Publicizing and Marketing Your Book

Your Roadmap to Becoming a Bestselling Author Congratulations—you're published! Whether you're promoting your first book or your fiftieth, *From Book to Bestseller* will help transform your marketing campaign from ordinary to extraordinary. *From Book to Bestseller* is your step-by-step guide to success. You'll learn how to plan and launch a super-savvy book-marketing program without breaking a sweat.

Here's what's inside:

- A step-by-step guide to developing the perfect publicity plan for your book

- How to get on radio and TV—today!

- Planning a super-successful book signing

- The secrets to crafting an exceptional press kit

- How to sell thousands of books through specialty retailers

- How to get your book into book clubs

- How to launch a successful publicity campaign on the Internet

ISBN: 1600370896 Paperback

Page Count: 250 pages

Genre: Nonfiction – Marketing

Pub Date: Spring 2015

Price: $29.95 Hardcover – $18.95 Paperback – $39.95 CD Audio

Format: Paperback – Hardcover – Audio

Trim: 6 x 9

Page Count: 296

Marketing and Publicity Information: Extensive Internet promotion including a Virtual Author Tour™, advance launch planned for *From Book to Bestseller* with top fifty book reviewers in print media, promotional push into publishing media (print and broadcast), book-club submission, book-review campaign, freelance article submission, announcement to author's mailing list of five thousand speaking engagements already booked for 2015

About the Author

Penny is a book-marketing and media-relations specialist. She coaches authors on projects, manuscripts, and marketing plans and instructs a variety of courses on publishing and promotion. Her company, Author Marketing Experts, Inc., specializes in nontraditional promotion for exceptional results. You can visit her website at www.amarketingexpert.com.

Must Do's before Pitching to Reviewers

No matter how compelling your book and pitch, you can only go so far if you haven't taken care of the basics. And nothing is more basic than a website. You have one, right? You should, and your site should be easy to read and navigate. You don't need fancy graphics or inspiring music: a clean, professional design and easy-to-find features are all you need. Your home page should include your book cover, book synopsis, a buy-this-book-now button, and links to interior pages on your site where visitors can learn more.

These interior pages should include an author's page with a bio. You may include a longer bio but have a short version—about 250 words—ready to use for reviews, press releases, and pitches. Also, have a nice downloadable photo reviewers or media can use. The shot should be in focus (you may say "duh," but we've seen plenty of author websites with blurry photos), professional, and not have a lot of clutter in the background. You should also have a high-quality, downloadable book-cover photo available. Some of the other pages and items you'll want to include are outlined below:

- A page for reviewers, blurbs, and testimonials, updated as soon as you have new material.

- A book excerpt may not be required, but it's highly recommended. Given how competitive review space is, this is something that can make the difference between a review request and a polite "No, thank you." Include the link to the excerpt in your pitch and press release (PR) for the book so it's easily accessible.

- A page with links to buy your book. List all applicable sites and include a way for visitors to click through them and make purchases.

- A page with contact information. If you're an expert on a timely, in-the-news topic, or want to make it easy for the media to find you, include a phone number as well as your e-mail address.

- Links to articles or blogs you've written.

The idea is to make it as easy as possible for prospective interviewers or reviewers to learn all about you and your book.

Bells and whistles won't cover for a weak website—ensuring that the basics are there so visitors can learn all about you and your book (and buy it) is critical. Visitors only spend seconds visiting websites; if they don't see what they need or want, they move on. Make your site inviting and informative so they'll stick around.

Find More Reviewers

In addition to pitching to reviewers, consider pitching to bloggers, too—it's a great way to get publicity and to find more reviewers. It's important to understand the differences between these two ways to harvest reviews. While pitching to reviewers can lead to coverage at any time (unless you've worked out a time frame with the reviewer), a blog tour typically covers your book for a specified time frame by a specified number of bloggers. On a blog tour an author goes from blog to blog instead of from store to store as on a traditional book tour. Depending on the author and the blog, tours generally last a week to a month and consist of reviews, interviews, guest posts, and giveaways.

Be sure to do your homework before jumping on a tour. First, figure out exactly what you'd like to do during your tour. For example, you may not want to write a lot of guest posts; many authors I know just don't have the time. In which case you'll want to limit your availability or offer book excerpts instead. In most cases, however, with interviews or guest blog posts, most bloggers will give you plenty of time. Second, figure out how long you'd like the tour to go (so you know how many bloggers you'll need), keep in mind here though that you may be at the mercy of a very busy blogger schedule so there's that, too. A good rule of thumb here is to have guest posts ready to go then let your research will uncover the best prospects to pitch to. Some bloggers love blog tours, others don't. Just give yourself plenty of time to set up your tour—bloggers are busy and will sometimes decline due to other commitments, so you'll want to have others in place.

As you set up your tour, you'll want to get each blogger's name, contact information, and preferred genres. If your genre is a natural fit for them, you can use that in your pitch. Also, become familiar with their style. Some bloggers emphasize only the positive, and if they can't say anything nice, they may decline to review the book. Others prefer to be honest (sometimes brutally), but most bloggers will reach out to the author and give them the option of not posting a negative review. Bloggers know how tough it is out there and will rarely slam a book unless there's something hideously wrong with it. As you peruse the blogs you're targeting, get a sense of their tone *before* approaching them. And honestly ask yourself how you'd feel having your book reviewed in that tone. If you can't handle it, don't pitch to that blogger. There are hundreds of blogs to pitch to, so be choosy.

And trust your instincts. You may find a gem of a blog with a low Google page rank, but if it's a nice-looking site, the posts are well-written, has regular commenters, and basically demonstrates a commitment to reviewing books, make a pitch!. Once you find blogs you like, look at their blog rolls for additional blogs to check out—often bloggers who like similar books list each other's websites.

Crafting the Perfect Book-Review Pitch

Once you've built a list of reviewers, it's time to start pitching. While this may not be as difficult as achieving world peace, it's amazing how many authors make serious mistakes at this stage. You just can't afford to do that. With thousands of books being published each year, competition for reviews is fierce. The average new book, if not heavily promoted by one of the major New York publishing houses, is not likely to get much in the way of newspaper or magazine reviews. That kind of review space has been shrinking for years, anyway. Meanwhile, there has been considerable growth in book blogging and online reviewing, though even with this growth, far more books are being published than there are bloggers available to review them. Understand that most reviewers do this as a labor of love and make little or no money. Their review blogs are not full-time endeavors but something they work into their already-busy lives. Learning how to make a great first impression in blog pitching is vital.

Fiction and nonfiction authors often take different approaches when pitching. For fiction, seek bloggers who review books in your genre, but if your book covers topics you're an expert in, you may have some options. For instance, if you've heavily researched the history of a city or historical figure, you may find history buffs who may be open to reviewing your book. Sometimes it helps to brainstorm a list of topics from your book, fact or fiction, in order to generate ideas for what types of publications or bloggers or reviewers to target.

With nonfiction, you're an expert on the topic(s) at hand and should look for peers in those areas who can help you find reviewers. And as nonfiction is much more competitive, it's smart to turn competitors into allies. See if you can find ways to help them—and use that as part of your pitch. You never know what kind of partnerships you can develop if you don't ask.

Now, in pitching, whether in fiction or nonfiction, it makes all the difference when you're familiar with the most effective strategies. Most bloggers identify themselves somewhere on their blogs. If they don't sign their posts, the "about me" section usually has their name. Use it! When you use a blogger's name, one thing is instantly clear: you actually took the time to find out who you're pitching to. That's a big plus. Briefly introduce yourself, and then don't just ask them to review your book, give them a reason, but keep it short, sweet, and to the point. Your e-mail subject line should also be brief yet clear: "Review request: Name of Book/genre" is effective. You don't have room to write a novel on the subject line, and you want the recipient to know right away what your e-mail is about. Here's a sample of an effective pitch:

BONUS!

We have more pitch samples at the end of this book.

Dear Amy,

I'm Joe Smith, author of the historical fiction novel Under the Sun, *which was just published by XYZ. I see you loved* A New Day *by Jane Doe, and I think my book fits in well with that and other books you review. I'd love to send you a review copy. You can learn more about my book and me by visiting my website at www.joesmith.com.*

In addition to a fantastic pitch, be sure to include all the basic book information in your e-mail:

- Title

- Author

- Genre

- ISBN (the thirteen digit ISBN of your preferred format, hardcover or paperback)

- Publication date (month, year)

- Pages

- Price

- Publisher

- Your website link (this should also be included on your press release, which you'll send out with copies of your book).

During your research phase, you'll learn things about a blogger that will help you get a review request. For instance, if they love a particular author and your book is in a similar vein, you can put that in your pitch. If you're comfortable having a little fun with your pitch, by all means, do. I once saw a pitch for a frothy romance that asked potential reviewers if they'd like to sin with a duke—very catchy and appropriate for the book. But don't force it. If that's not your style, don't worry about it. It's far more important to explain who you are, what your book is about, why this reviewer should be interested in your book, and provide links to your website so they can learn more about your book and request a review copy. And when they follow up by clicking on your links, make sure whatever information they'll need is in place and easily accessible.

You may or may not hear back right away. Some bloggers check their e-mail daily, others weekly. Be patient. It's fine to follow up in a couple of weeks if you feel you matched up with a particular blog and haven't heard back. It's always possible that your original e-mail ended up in spam or was overlooked (the sheer volume of review requests reviewers receive is often staggering). After that, if there's still no word, move on. Seek reviews from other bloggers.

Turning Your Book into a 24/7 Sales Tool

Let your book go to work for you. You can use the book itself to encourage reviews. One of our clients, a first-time, unknown author, was ready to market her book. We knew that given her genre (contemporary romance), the potential for garnering reviews was low. So we decided to encourage reviews by having her write a request letter to her readers at the end of her book. In her letter, she politely asked for feedback and a review. She now has nearly seventy reviews on Amazon. Simple but effective! And remember, she was a first-time author with no online history—and she self-published. Even with all these things working against her, she got tons of reviews. Were they all five-star? No, but let's face it, a book page populated with tons of five-star reviews is suspect anyway. All of the reviews are authentic, written by real readers the author became engaged with. What's more, these readers are now part of her "tribe." She stays in touch with them and lets them know whenever another one of her books comes out.

For her second book, we encouraged her to actually write a letter explaining how tough it can be to get reviews and encouraging her readers to review her book(s) on Amazon. She also thanked them for buying her book. The result was amazing. Here's the letter if you'd like to try it out for yourself. (Feel free to copy it or revise it—whatever you feel works for you—but use it. It works!)

Thank you for reading!

Dear Reader,

I hope you enjoyed *Shelf Life: The Publicist*, book 2. I have to tell you, I really love the characters Mac and Kate. Many readers wrote me asking, "What's next for Nick?" Well, be sure to stay tuned because the saga of publishing drama isn't quite over. Nick will be back in book 3. Will he find his happy ending? I sure hope so.

When I wrote *The Publicist*, book 1, I got many letters from fans thanking me for the book. Some had opinions about Mac and Kate, while others rooted for Nick. As an author, I love feedback. Candidly, you're the reason I will explore Nick's future. So tell me what you liked, what you loved, even what you hated. I'd love to hear from you. You can write me at authorchristinageorge@gmail.com and visit me on the web at www.thepublicistnovel.com.

Finally, I need to ask a favor. If you're so inclined, I'd love a review of *Shelf Life*. Loved it, hated it—I'd just enjoy your feedback. Reviews can be tough to come by these days, and you, the reader, have the power to make or break a book. If you have the time, here's a link to my author page, along with all my books on Amazon: http://amzn.to/19p3dNx

Thank you so much for reading *Shelf Life* and for spending time with me.

In gratitude,

Christina George

Just a few things about this letter. First, you can't ask for just good reviews. Second, a lot of people may read this as an ebook, so be sure to put a live link in the book, preferably a link to your Amazon Author Central page, because when you're putting your book together, you won't have the actual link to the Amazon page it's on, and of course you want your readers to see all of your books, not just the one they're reading. Be sure to add this letter to the last page of your book, not the front matter. A lot of authors like to write letters to their readers, but that's not the purpose here. You want to thank them for reading a book they just finished. If your request is at the front, they'll forget about it by the time they get to the end.

The Benefits of Cross-Promotion

Another way to engage readers is to draw them from one book to the other. Generally, when you are reading a book on Kindle and you get to the end of the book, it will send you over to the book's page and ask you to rate it. One thing the Kindle device doesn't do is send readers to the author's Author Central page, where they can see the author's other books. Kindle's in the business of selling books, so referring you to the "Also bought" page makes more sense for them, but that's not true for you. Cross-promoting your books is an invaluable strategy for drawing readers to your books.

Here are some ways you can cross-promote your books:

- List your other titles at the back of your book. If you have too many, pick two or three and vary which ones you mention in each of your books, meaning that in book X you reference titles A and B, and in book Y you mention books C and D.

- Include a book excerpt or excerpts with the book mentions.

- Create a special offer that links to your website or, ideally, a special page on your site that takes your reader to your special offer. Maybe as a thank-you, give them a free download of one of your books or special reports. In exchange for this freebie you get their e-mail address. This does two things: first, the freebie builds goodwill with your reader, and second, you're collecting their e-mail for future promotions.

BONUS TIP!

Get a URL that best describes your niche. For me it's www. SellMorebooksonAmazon.com. This URL forwards searchers to my Amazon Author Central page so, in the future, any reference to that URL will forward to that page and also to my books.

How to Find the Top Amazon Reviewers

There's no doubt finding reviewers who review regularly for Amazon is a great thing. Many of these folks review hundreds of books on Amazon per year, and with that comes a lot of credibility.

So how do you get these all-important reviews? You can do this a couple of ways. Some of your reviews will come through networking, others from plain old research. Let's take a look at the Amazon reviewer page; this is where the top reviewers are listed:

http://www.amazon.com/review/top-reviewers

As you can see, the list has two tabs on it, Top Reviewer Rankings and Hall of Fame Reviewers. The Hall of Fame list is really the top of the top. If you can get picked up by one of these folks, you're golden. It's not easy, but it can be done. Also keep in mind that this list can be confusing because these top reviewers don't always review books (they may review products instead). You need to check each individually to see what they review. First, click on their name, which pulls up their reviewer page. Amazon has recently reformatted these so they're much easier to peruse:

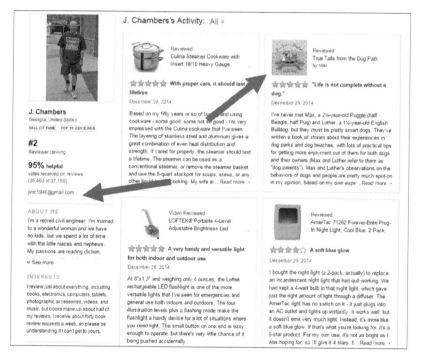

As you can see from his profile, J. Chambers reviews a lot of different things for Amazon, including books (see red arrow on the right, above), and he doesn't just review kids' books. Farther down the page you'll see he's done coffee table books as well as fiction, so if your book fits that profile, he may be a good person to pitch to.

Additionally, when you click on a reviewer's profile, it'll have information about them and often will indicate what they will and won't review when it comes to books. One reviewer profile said, "I no longer review ebooks," which goes back to our earlier discussion about the saturation of the ebook market and why having multiple formats is smart.

Another way to find reviewers is to look at books with similar titles to yours. You can also search books that cover the same or similar topics. Take a look at who's reviewed their books. Let's say you're looking at Grady Harp, a Hall of Fame reviewer on Amazon, and you see his reviews and think, "Wow, he'd love my book, too," so you follow the link to his Amazon profile page, get his e-mail, and send him a pitch. Although it's takes a little effort to go this route, it's 100 percent worth it. If you start early (i.e., before your book is published), you'll be able to target these folks as soon as your book is ready to go. Here's a snapshot of what it might look like, from my own book: *Red Hot Internet Publicity*, and John Chancellor, who is a top five-hundred reviewer at Amazon:

If you click on John's name, it will take you to his profile, e-mail, and pitching guidelines. It's that easy. Just remember to follow the guidelines in this book and keep your pitches short and sweet.

The Secret to Doubling the Amount of Review Requests You Receive

Last year I conducted an experiment to see if I could double or triple the reviews I could get if I were an unknown, newly published author. If you've ever tried to get reviews, you know it's tough for a first-time author. You're lucky to get one or two at most. I always tell authors to personalize their pitches. Most of the time they sort of nod in agreement, but I suspect few actually do it because it can be time intensive. Not only do you have to go to the reviewer's blog, find their name, look up some of the books they've reviewed, decide if they're right for your book, and then pitch to them, but to ensure your success, you need to take it a step further. Find and include some personal information about your reviewer, too. For example, I was pitching to a reviewer and noticed that she had a dog named Library, so I included that in my pitch. It personalizes it and shows that you're paying attention, which is important! Whenever I did this, I tripled and even quadrupled the number of review requests I got for this unknown author.

Personalizing each e-mail may seem tedious and time-consuming, but sending out hundreds of e-mails that receive no response, not getting reviews for a book, and selling less is infinitely worse. All this initial legwork paves the path for future success in this market. And if you keep a list of these e-mail contacts in an Excel document, when you publish to this market again, your one-time effort will be maximized. You won't have to redo the research, and you can pull from the list you already have. Relationships take time, but you'll find that if you've already built them for the first book, getting reviews for the second takes half the time.

How to Respond to a Review

Most of the time when we get reviews, they're good. Sometimes they're even great. Occasionally, though, you may get a review that's not so great. Unfortunately, not everyone will love your book. When that happens, just let it go, but before you do, thank that reviewer for reading it anyway. They may ask you if you still want them to run the review. The choice is yours, of course, but unless it's really bad and meant to be hurtful, every review deserves a response.

How to Respond to Reviews on Author Central

When you log onto your Author Central account, look for the blue bar at the top. You'll see a button for customer reviews.

This button will take you to the page shown below, where you'll see a bunch of your reviews. Under each review you'll see the "Add a comment" button, where you can respond to reviews. It's a great way to connect with your readers on Amazon!

Here's a screenshot:

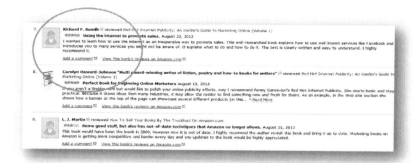

Review Incentives

If you have a gift that ties into your product—swag—it's totally fine to send that to the reviewer. Seriously. Reviewers *love* swag (as long as it's classy and not junk). Incentives can be a great way to pull in readers, so send swag with your book. We offered a book-themed tote bag for the first twenty-five reviews on one book and ended up getting almost all twenty-five reviews overnight because fans were so eager for the tote bag. Just make sure you tell your reviewers you want an honest review, good or bad.

And keep it on the up and up, unlike the guy who in desperation to get reviews offered an all-expenses-paid cruise for the best review, with no intention of actually following through. While this wasn't illegal, it was unethical. The author got a lot of reviews, but he also got several people posting reviews on his Amazon page that called out his scam. Not a good way to get reviews.

One of the best incentives you can offer your readers is to express sincere gratitude. Always, always, always send a thank-you either with the book or after. Even if you don't like the review, thank them anyway. You'll cast your net even wider if you do. Reviewers talk. Be grateful no matter what. They'll really appreciate that.

Gifting eBooks

- Gifting ebooks is fun way to use the Amazon.com system. You can gift ebooks to reviewers who request a MOBI (Kindle-formatted) copy of the book, or you can gift them to various readers to help generate buzz and drive sales. Be sure to drop the price of the book before gifting, though, because the gifting process will cost you less if you do. I generally drop the price of my book to ninety-nine cents before gifting. And while it'd be nice to gift your book during your freebie giveaway time, Amazon won't let you. The book has to be at a certain price point—whatever pricing you determine.

- Gifting a book does not necessarily mean that everyone will actually download your book. They can actually use the price of the book to buy something else. That's why I keep the pricing low—so it's too much work to flip it into something else and much more appealing to download your book.

- When you gift the book, Amazon will send you to a form you can fill out with any message you want. Just complete and hit send.

- You will be charged per book you send, but you will *not* get paid royalties until the recipient downloads it, which means that if they don't see the e-mail notification (if it winds up in spam or whatever), you'll still get charged but won't get your cut. You can circumvent this problem by sending the book to people you actually know. That way they'll be more inclined to grab it. Also, be sure to send them an e-mail in advance to let them know it's coming.

Gifting ebooks can help spike sales especially if everyone is downloading the book on the same day. And as a final tip, if you want to spike your book in a particular category, encourage your friends or followers to download immediately so it'll have a greater impact on your Amazon presence!

Harnessing the Power of Goodreads

During the past year, Goodreads has become a front-and-center social network for authors; first, with their new Amazon relationship (Amazon purchased Goodreads in 2013), and now they've doubled their readership to twenty million. Though many authors and publishers vowed to close their Goodreads accounts after the merger, it seems Goodreads is still going strong and maintaining its independence. Goodreads CEO Otis Chandler cites three primary factors behind this acceleration: "a critical mass of book reviews," "explosive" mobile growth, and international expansion. If you're not on Goodreads or if you haven't touched your account in a while, you should consider the benefits this site offers.

There are many success stories about authors who "got noticed" there, mingling with other members and getting tons of reviews. While success isn't guaranteed, Goodreads can help you get a leg up on your promotion.

To know what does and doesn't work on Goodreads, it helps to understand the average demographic of the site: adult females, many with college-age kids, and surprisingly, a whopping 81 percent Caucasian. They are avid readers, though many are less affluent than the average Internet user, so low-priced books and free books do well on this site.

As an author, your number-one goal on Goodreads should be to get reviews. Some of the most successful authors and books that were once "dark horses" came up in the ranks through the power of Goodreads, both for reader engagement and for reviews. Goodreads reviews work harder than most reviews. They are syndicated to USA Today.com, e-commerce sites, and library-related sites. One note on Goodreads reviews: you may get slammed with negative reviews. Reviewers and readers sometimes go to war on Goodreads. If someone doesn't like your book, let it go. It's a much trickier walk if you start to fight a reviewer who has a huge following battling right along with her. Stay positive. Not everyone will like your book, even on Goodreads, but the potential for publicity is worth the risk.

Here are a few tips for getting more reviews on Goodreads:

- Post excerpts of your book on your page.

- Create a blog post that says your book is available for review, and provide a link to your blog on your page.

- Use groups to get reviewed on Goodreads.

- Make sure your website has a Goodreads widget. When you sign up for your account, you'll see where and how to get these widgets. It's a great way to attract an additional following.

- Schedule a Goodreads giveaway.

Goodreads Newsletters

Goodreads offers a couple of newsletters to help you stay in touch with the community, what's trending, etc.

The first is the Goodreads Author-focused ezine. This fantastic newsletter, though not published with any regular frequency (or as often as their main newsletter), often has great marketing tips, ideas for promotion on Goodreads, and website shortcuts. It's worth the sign-up: http://www.goodreads.com/author/newsletter. Their regular monthly newsletter can be found here: http://www. goodreads.com/newsletter. A lot of advertising opportunities are found within this newsletter, and although their webpage advertising does fairly well, I have no current data on how well the ads in their newsletters do, so if you decide to advertise in the newsletters, proceed with caution.

Your Goodreads Profile

When you first start with Goodreads, you'll be a "user." Once you have a user profile, you can upgrade to an author profile. There are a lot of articles out there on creating a great profile on Goodreads. Just be sure to include a professional headshot. And don't leave any of the areas on your profile blank; fill in the "about you" section, "books you like to read" section, etc. Here's a quick link to the author profile info on Goodreads: http://www.goodreads.com/ author/program.

Adding your blog to your profile is a fantastic way to promote yourself on the page. Your readers will get to know you as you consistently post good content. Also, it's a good bit of "SEO juice" with your followers because a blog post on Goodreads generates a link (and hopefully traffic) back to your website. Simply add your blog feed by clicking on the drop-down arrow, then "edit profile" next to your picture (at the top right-hand side of the page).

Also, if you have a book video or author video, be sure to promote it on Goodreads. It's easy to add video once you're in the profile settings. Also, it's best to pull the video directly from YouTube (upload it there if you haven't already) instead of from your website. In most cases website hosting services will charge mega fees to host videos if you're trying to host it on your site. Also it's never a bad idea to have a YouTube account since video is a big social media tool.

Goodreads Groups

Groups can be great places to network. Some will even let you request book reviews. Goodreads has thousands of groups. Try to join at least one or two right off the bat. You can add more later as you get used to navigating the system.

To sign up for groups, simply start searching for them. In deciding on the right group, consider a few things, like genre and how much activity the group sees. And look for a group that's robust and active, so you don't waste your time. Additionally, you can jump ship. If you find the activity isn't right for you, join another group or groups. You can always sign up for the original group again later. As far as I've been able to tell, Goodreads does not have a limit on the amount of groups you can join, but it's smart to join only those you can participate in, otherwise it's like showing up for a fabulous party and watching from the sidewalk. It won't do you much good, and it can get pretty cold.

When you join a group, it's important to remember that, first and foremost, you are a reader, not a promoter. While you're there to publicize your book, launching into self-promotion right off the bat is not recommended—it could get you banned from some exceptional groups if you're not careful. Your goal is to be "helpful," so join in on a discussion. Engage first, promote later.

- If the group has freebie days (days when you can announce your Goodreads giveaway), take advantage of them. If not, don't announce your giveaway. If you aren't sure, ask the group moderator(s) for their input.

- Most groups have a bookshelf. If you want your book placed on this shelf, ask the moderator. Though, here again, it's wise to become a contributing member before you put them on the shelf.

- Participate in things like polls and roundtable discussions. The key to getting noticed in these groups is discussion. If you're not participating, you're just sitting on the sideline watching everyone else.

Finally, you can also create your own group. It's called the Featured Author Group, open only to Goodreads authors. Readers can discuss your book, its topics, your writing, and anything related to your book. It's a fantastic vehicle for sharing with your readers, getting to know them, and growing your base. To start your own group, go here: http://www.goodreads.com/author/featured_groups

A couple fantastic Goodreads groups to join are listed below. Both allow you to highlight your book and request reviews.

http://www.goodreads.com/group/show/60696-making-connections

http://www.goodreads.com/group/show/26989-goodreads-authors-readers

A Quick and Simple Action List for Goodreads

In order to build your presence on Goodreads, you'll need to be active. This doesn't mean you need to be on the site daily. If you can, great, but if not, that's fine too. But at least once a week:

- Add a new book to your shelves—one you're reading, one you want to read, or a book that inspired your writing.

- Write a review for someone else's book. If you do a lot of Amazon reviews, you can simply repost that content to Goodreads. And to make yourself the real "darling" of the review world, grab your Goodreads review and cross-post it to Amazon. Wouldn't you love it if someone did that for you?

- Rate books. It's easy. You don't even have to write a review; just give stars.

- Blog post. If you update your blog weekly, that's fantastic; if you don't, at least update your Goodreads status once a week. It doesn't have to be a long post. You can just add a favorite book passage or an author quote. You're aiming for profile activity.

- Post to a group, make a comment, or respond to someone's question.

- Add friends at least weekly. You'll find people in groups that you want to friend or reviews you want to follow. Building a healthy friend list is key to expanding your network (and getting more reviews) on Goodreads.

The Power of the Goodreads Giveaways

One of the best ways to kick-start book discovery is with a Goodreads giveaway. I recommend doing multiple giveaways for a book. Even prepublication giveaways will help spike success and reviews on the site.

While most folks recommend long giveaways (i.e., thirty days), I recommend you run them for shorter periods. A week to ten days is optimal because your giveaway drops off the new-giveaways list quickly but it's also put on a list of those ending soon. So if you do a shorter giveaway, you'll likely be on the "ending soon" list since it covers giveaways ending in twenty-four to forty-eight hours. Be sure to post an update about this on your Goodreads page and on your blog, especially if your blog is connected to your Goodreads page.

So how many books should you give away? I've done anywhere from ten to fifty, but it's best to keep it lower. Ten is manageable; fifty becomes unruly. While a higher number sounds great, at some point you will have to fill the order, and Goodreads only allows printed books. Since you can't give an ebook or PDF version, you'll have to mail print books (you can also ship them from Amazon).

If you're a member of a few groups, there's likely a thread to promote a giveaway, so find that thread and post to it. Regardless of your giveaway time frame, post it once at the beginning and again as you're nearing the end. I'm not a fan of blasting groups with "all about me" posts, so twice is my limit. You may find groups that encourage more frequent giveaway reminders, but I doubt it. Other authors on the site are trying to get attention too.

You can even use giveaways with your older books. There aren't any Goodreads rules against it. If you have a great book and are just discovering this site, do a giveaway and see what happens—especially if it's not your only book and you're writing new material. Some authors with multiple titles start with their oldest books and work their way forward.

Whether your book is new or old, if you want to maximize your exposure on Goodreads, let your contest run internationally. You'll get better participation that way, and in the big picture, global shipping isn't really that expensive.

Ready to sign up for your own giveaway? Then head over here: www.goodreads.com/giveaway. Once there, be ready to list the start and end dates as well as all pertinent book information such as ISBN, book description, publisher, and number of copies you're willing to give away. Then you're ready to go with your first Goodreads giveaway!

When the campaign is over, the system will send you a spreadsheet with the winners, their Goodreads IDs, and their addresses. Be sure to congratulate the winners on Goodreads and let them know you're shipping the book out—another great way to connect with the person on the receiving end of your book. And it helps encourage a review from the reader. You're no longer an anonymous writer; you're connected on Goodreads and following one another's reviews, etc. Reach out to everyone who entered, thanking them for entering the contest and for their interest.

Whenever I do a Goodreads giveaway, I include a short, handwritten note as I mail the book, congratulating the person on winning and thanking them for their participation. Instead of asking for a review in the note, I encourage their feedback because I really want to know what the reader thinks of the book. Then I give them my e-mail address in case they want to make direct contact. A personal note is key in connecting with and engaging your readers. I also sign each of the books I give away. Readers love signed books!

So how many reviews can you expect, really? Goodreads estimates that 60 percent of books given away get reviewed, but I've seen numbers both higher and lower. A lot of it depends on the book, of course. Good books get reviewed more frequently. Also, it seems fiction gets a lot more reviews, but it's not a given.

Another way to boost exposure is to run an ad to help push your giveaway. Ads are simple on Goodreads. They operate on a pay-per-click system, which means you only pay when someone clicks on your ad. You also buy credit, and I suggest starting at ten dollars. You can always add more, but you may never use $100. Get started here: http://www.goodreads.com/advertisers.

Goodreads openly admits that new ads that generate a lot of clicks in the first few days will be shown more frequently throughout the day—essentially Goodreads gives its users what they want. So make your ad content compelling, and don't go the super-cheap route when it comes to bidding on your per-click cost. The minimum is ten cents, the recommendation is usually fifty. Some say "go big or go home." I say do what you're comfortable with, but remember, higher per-click ads are given priority. Some additional insight into how Goodreads ads work can be found here: http://www.goodreads.com/help/list/advertisers/.

Try creating two ads, using different tactics. One could say something like "Enter to win"; the other something like "Get your FREE book." The words "win" and "free" are always hot. In the main content include a short, irresistible description of your book, something that makes it stand out, then close with "Giveaway ends [insert date]" to help encourage people to act. The link you include with your ad should be the link to your giveaway page. To find that link, go here: http://www.goodreads.com/giveaway. On the right-hand side of the page you'll see a section entitled, "Giveaways You've Created."

A few more giveaway tips:

- Let readers know if you plan on providing signed copies.

- End your giveaway on a nonpopular date, like the middle of the week; *not* on a holiday.

- Again, more countries equals more exposure.

- Mail your copies promptly.

Reach out to winners with a short, respectful follow-up. Friend them and let them know you'd love their input when they're ready.

And there's a bonus! When you're done creating your ad, you'll be given the HTML code for a giveaway widget you can add to your blog or website!

Using the power of free to help boost your book, especially on a site like Goodreads, is a great idea. It creates opportunities to connect with new readers and opens a dialogue about your book in general. So capitalize on this opportunity; you'll be glad you did!

How to Review Books

You may find this an odd chapter to include in a book about getting reviews, but posting them is important too. Over the years I've heard from numerous folks who have friends who post reviews on Amazon, for which they are grateful but wished they were more detailed. Many times the reviews consisted of "Loved this book!" And while it's great to have fans, it does little to help a book along.

When a book has lots of great, detailed reviews, we tend to scan them for highlights on the things that matter to us. That's how we often buy books. Both good and bad reviews can help us decide, and, frankly, I've often bought a book after I read a bad review because what the reviewer didn't like was exactly what I was looking for. That's why detailed reviews are not only helpful, they're a must for your Amazon page.

It's tempting to ask friends and family to write reviews. They often want to help but aren't sure what to say. And you may have readers who love your work but aren't savvy on posting reviews. Here are some tips you can share with those who want to post something about your book:

- Whenever possible or appropriate, ask the reviewer to add their expertise on the topic if your book relates to nonfiction.

- If you have identified your keywords, share them with any friends who are posting and ask them that, if appropriate, they include the keywords in the review.

- Ask readers to post reviews that are between 100 and 450 words.

- If a reader feels compelled to include a spoiler, ask them to post a warning first so the customer can chose to read on—or not.

- Never, ever, ever offer to edit a review. You want honest appraisals, not watered-down reviews that all sound alike.

- It's important that the reviewer cite why the book mattered to them. This also personalizes the review for the reader.

If your reviewer still isn't sure how to craft a review, here are some starter questions to help them along:

1. What did you like most about the book?

2. What about the book surprised you?

3. Did the book cover the content as described?

4. Do you think you got your money's worth?

5. What could the author have done better?

6. How does it compare to other books in this category? And please cite any books you'd compare this one to.

Bonus Resources

Check out this website for some great places to list your ebook freebie!

http://www.mediabistro.com/galleycat/15-places-to-promote-your-book-for-free_b76294

Here are some great bloggers to pitch to!

Mystery Bloggers

Cozy Mystery List: http://www.cozy-mystery.com/

Mystery Scene: http://www.mysteryscenemag.com

Detectives Beyond Borders: http://detectivesbeyondborders.blogspot.com/

Murder by the Book: http://mbtb-books.blogspot.com/

Murderati: http://www.murderati.com/

Mysteries in Paradise: http://paradise-mysteries.blogspot.com/

Mystery Fanfare: http://mysteryreadersinc.blogspot.com/

Shots: Crime & Thriller Ezine: http://www.shotsmag.co.uk/

Stop, You're Killing Me: http://www.stopyourekillingme.com/

Romance Bloggers

Reading Romances: http://reading-romances.com/

Romance Reviews Today: http://romrevtoday.blogspot.com/

Babbling About Books, and More: http://kbgbabbles.com/

Love Saves the World: http://lovesavestheworld.blogspot.mx

Nocturne Romance Reads: http://www.nocturnereads.com

Not Another Romance Blog: http://notanotherromanceblog.blogspot.com

Penelope's Romance Reviews: http://www.pennyromance.com/

The Romance Reviews: http://theromancereviews.blogspot.com/

Business Bloggers

Brazen Life: http://blog.brazencareerist.com/

B2C: Business 2 Community: http://www.business2community.com/

BUSINESS INSIDER: http://www.businessinsider.com/

SmartBlog on Leadership: https://smartblogs.com/category/leadership/

Success: http://www.success.com/

Inc.: http://www.inc.com/

the Daily Muse: http://www.thedailymuse.com/

TLNT: http://www.tlnt.com/

Young Entrepreneur: http://www.youngentrepreneur.com/blog/

Under 30 CEO: http://under30ceo.com/

Book Reviewers on the Web

This list includes industry standards, literary blogs, off-the-beaten-track blogs, and the more opinion-driven book bloggers: http://robinmizell.wordpress.com/book-reviewers/.

- **Midwest Book Review** (lists a number of sites to check out) http://www.midwestbookreview.com/links/othr_rev.htm

- **Best of the Web blogs** (blog listing with a description of each blog listed) http://blogs.botw.org/Arts/Literature/Book_Reviews/

- **YA Book Blog Directory** (bloggers who specialize in young adult books) http://yabookblogdirectory.blogspot.com/p/ya-book-blogger-list.html

- **Kidlitosphere Central** (bloggers of children's and young adult literature) http://www.kidlitosphere.org/bloggers/

- **FSB** (search by genre for bloggers who review those kinds of books) http://www.fsbmedia.com/book_blogger_search.php

- **Book Blogs Search** (a huge listing of blogs) http://fyrefly-books.wordpress.com/about/book-blogs-search/

More Great Resources

- **About blog book tours**: http://blogbooktours.blogspot.com/2010/06/blog-tips-to-consider.html

- **Writing an effective cover letter:** http://www.midwest-bookreview.com/bookbiz/advice/cvr-ltr.htm

- **Writing an effective publicity release**: http://www.mid-westbookreview.com/bookbiz/advice/prelease.htm

Get More Readers!

Remind people they don't need a Kindle to access ebooks. Whenever you do a book promo, mention that readers can access your book through all of these resources:

Kindle Cloud Reader: https://read.amazon.com/about

iPhone and iPad apps: http://www.amazon.com/gp/feature.html/ref=kcp_iph_ln_ar?docId=1000301301

Android app: http://www.amazon.com/gp/feature.html/ref=kcp_and_ln_ar?docId=165849822

BlackBerry app: http://www.amazon.com/gp/feature.html/ref=klm_lnd_inst?docId=1000468551

Pitching Tips

When pitching to media, here are a few things to keep in mind:

- Always include a recipient name. If you can't find the person you're looking for, then send it to the managing editor, though usually it's easy to find a recipient's name on the company's website or by doing a simple Internet search.

- Always keep the pitch to one page.

- Always include your website URL.

- Always include a review (or partial review), if you have one, from a legit source.

- Always tell them what you want—a review, feature, interview opportunity, etc.

- Always sign your letters.

- Always include a book if you can afford it. And really, you can afford it!

Tips for pitching via e-mail:

- Always attach an image of the front cover.

- When crafting a subject, be straightforward or you'll risk sounding like spam.

- Always let them know you're happy to mail them a book or gift one via Amazon.

Tips for fiction:

- Always include an intriguing opening paragraph. Don't just say, "I have a book."

- When describing your story, highlight the points that make your book unique.

- Leave a cliffhanger. You want them to want to find out what happens.

- Print your letter on letterhead if you have a business or company related to your published work.

Sample fiction e-mail subject:
"For review: New book takes you inside the publishing industry"

Tips for nonfiction:

- Always include an intriguing opening paragraph. List the name of your book, the market it pertains to, and what makes it unique.

- Always include selling points. Lists, bullets, etc., of features in the book that make it better than anything else on the market are key!

- If you have a tips sheet of your own, a top-ten list, a single-page how-to, etc., include that with your pitch letter. This is another opportunity to show what kind of content you're producing and may convince them to open your book.

- Print your letter on your business or company letterhead.

Sample nonfiction e-mail subject:
"For review: The insider's guide to marketing online"

Sample Letters

Date

Recipient name
Outlet or publication
Address
City, state, zip

Dear Name,

I have recently released the one marketing book every author and business owner must have in their arsenal, *Red Hot Internet Publicity: The Insider's Guide to Marketing Online.*

Authors, speakers and small business owners have three choices these days, they can:

1. Spend a fortune on advertising and other old-school marketing and pray they'll make back their investment—against all odds.

2. Fritter away two or three years blindly stumbling around, trying to figure out what works on their own while competing for attention with more than 25 billion web pages.

3. Listen to an expert who will show them how to get their website noticed, visited, and purchased from, an expert who can show them how to be smart and successful online while keeping their dollars in their own wallet, and whose own site is in the top 1 percent of all the sites in the world for traffic.

"Packed with wisdom, insights, advice, and how-tos, this book should be considered your social media bible . . . no marketing effort is complete without it." —Rick Frishman, Founder, Planned Television Arts PR/Publisher, Morgan James Books

If you would like to learn more, please visit www.amarketingexpert.com.

I appreciate your time and hope you'll consider reviewing *Red Hot Internet Publicity*. Please don't hesitate to contact me with any questions or additional requests.

Sincerely,

Your name

Date

Recipient name
Outlet or publication
Address
City, state, zip

Dear Name,

Welcome to the world of publishing. The ego has landed. Can one woman change an age-old institution like publishing? Probably not, but in my newly released book, *The Publicist*, Kate Mitchell sure wants to try.

As a publicist with a large, respected New York publishing house, Kate finds herself at the mercy of a broken publishing system, books that don't sell, and author egos that are often, well, as big as the island of Manhattan. Enter the star editor, MacDermott Ellis—tall, handsome, charismatic, married, and ready to save the day. Then there's Allan Lavigne, once a revered author—now as forgotten as last year's bestsellers, and his nephew Nick—tall, gorgeous, sweet, single, and ready to sweep Kate off her feet. Kate wants to do the right thing, but her hormones seem to be driving her decisions.

As Kate tries to navigate the landmine of publicity, over-the-top author expectations, and the careful dance of "I'm sorry, your book isn't on the bestseller list this week," she also finds authors who are painfully overlooked by a publisher wanting more sex, more celebrities, and more scandal.

"I've often imagined what it must be like to work in this industry . .
. I'm sure Ms. George has more than a few industry insiders chuckling at her stories *and* cringing at how close to home they hit . . . I
think *The Publicist* is a nice tease of what I'm hoping will be much
more to come from Ms. George." —Scandalicious Book Reviews

If you would like to learn more, please visit www.thepublicistnovel.com.

I appreciate your time and hope you'll consider reviewing *The
Publicist*. Please don't hesitate to contact me with any questions or
additional requests.

Sincerely,

Christina George

Are you selling enough books on Amazon.com?

If you're not sure, or if your answer is a definite "No!" then we have a simple solution: the Amazon Optimization Program, offered exclusively through Author Marketing Experts, Inc.

What most authors don't realize is that Amazon is a search engine—and it needs to be treated like a search engine—not simply an online bookstore. So what does that mean? Keywords are important, and most authors don't have the time or the knowledge to configure their keywords properly. You also need to know how Amazon algorithms work.

Luckily, we know how they work and how Amazon is "triggered" to push books onto your readers' radar screens.

So we've designed a program to share this knowledge, to find the perfect keywords and the exact right categories for your book!

Find out more at http://bit.ly/AmazonOptimizationProgramInfo

And be sure to use this code to get 50% off: 2015PROMO50

PENNY C. SANSEVIERI

For more books by Penny, go to: www.SellMorebooksonAmazon.com

Thanks for reading! If you have the time, I'd really love a review: www.SellMorebooksonAmazon.com, Reviews are a huge help to authors, so thank you in advance.

Wishing you much success!

About Penny C. Sansevieri & Author Marketing Experts, Inc.

Penny C. Sansevieri, founder and CEO Author Marketing Experts, Inc. (AME), is a bestselling author and internationally recognized book-marketing and media-relations expert. She is an adjunct professor of self-publishing at NYU.

Her company is a leader in the publishing industry and has developed some of the most innovative social media and Internet book-marketing campaigns. She is author of five books, including *Red Hot Internet Publicity*, which has been called "the leading guide to everything Internet."

AME is the first book-marketing and publicity firm to use Internet promotion to its full impact through the Virtual Author Tour™, which strategically harnesses social networking sites such as Twitter, blogs, book videos, and other relevant resources to push an author's message into the online community on sites related to the book's topic, and thereby position the author in his or her market.

PENNY C. SANSEVIERI

AME has had eleven books recently top bestseller lists, including *New York Times*, *USA Today*, and *Wall Street Journal* lists.

To learn more about Penny's books or her promotional services, visit her website at www.amarketingexpert.com.

Made in the USA
Middletown, DE
29 January 2016